THE WIDOWER'S NOTEBOOK

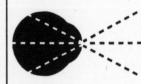

This Large Print Book carries the
Seal of Approval of N.A.V.H.

THE WIDOWER'S NOTEBOOK

A MEMOIR

JONATHAN SANTLOFER

THORNDIKE PRESS

A part of Gale, a Cengage Company

Farmington Hills, Mich • San Francisco • New York • Waterville, Maine
Meriden, Conn • Mason, Ohio • Chicago

LIBRARY OF CONGRESS CIP DATA ON FILE.
CATALOGUING IN PUBLICATION FOR THIS BOOK
IS AVAILABLE FROM THE LIBRARY OF CONGRESS

ISBN-13: 978-1-4328-5751-6 (hardcover)

Published in 2019 by arrangement with Penguin Books, an imprint of Penguin Publishing Group, a division of Penguin Random House LLC

Printed in Mexico
1 2 3 4 5 6 7 23 22 21 20 19

*For Joy Santlofer: wife, mother,
sister, writer, friend.
You are greatly missed.*

*And for our daughter, Doria,
the brightest light.*

Between grief and nothing,
I will take grief.

— WILLIAM FAULKNER

HOW TO BEGIN

Do I start with the part where I am paralyzed, back pressed hard against the living room wall, shrinking into it but watching as if through a lens zooming in and out of the action, near then far, all of it taking place no more than five, six feet in front of me, firemen pushing the coffee table aside, books toppling, paramedics rolling my wife onto the floor, one tearing open her blouse and searching for a heartbeat, another pressing her chest up and down as a second team races in and a woman takes over, flips open a black bag and inserts a tube down my wife's throat, everything happening in hyperspeed, while I stare at my wife's face gone pale and the room going gray and grainy as an old photograph?

Or, do I start ten, twenty minutes earlier, impossible to track the time, when I come into the living room and even from twenty feet away I can see that something is terribly wrong, my wife, Joy, on the couch, beckoning to me, mouth open but unable to speak, her eyes large and terrified, and I rush to her side and she grips my arm and I pull her to me and frantically attempt to dial 911, trying to punch in three simple numbers but can't get them right, as my wife gasps for breath and I say over and over, *"Take it easy, honey — breathe — hang on — you'll be okay,"* trying hard to sound comforting and rational, as a voice comes on the phone and I say, "My wife, she's not breathing —" and the woman on the other end, speaking calmly — *How is that possible?* — asks my name and address and I am shouting now *"Hurry! — Please!"* and minutes later — I think it's minutes — time is spiraling, collapsing — firemen and paramedics burst on the scene, push the coffee table aside, and roll my wife onto the floor and tear open her blouse, while I am backed up against the living room wall, watching the unwatchable: watching my wife die.

PART I
BEFORE

1
NOTHING OUT OF
THE ORDINARY

Joy went into the hospital on a Thursday morning in mid-August, a torn ligament or tendon of the knee, a torn meniscus to be specific. Outpatient surgery. *No big deal,* that's what the doctor said. She had torn it walking up (or was it down?) a flight of stairs at the Museum of Modern Art, and limped around for weeks until finally making the decision to have surgery.

The night before we binge-watched *Episodes,* the Matt LeBlanc TV series. It had become a favorite, and we loved watching and rewatching it when either one of us was in a bad mood or feeling anxious, and Joy *was* anxious, though I kept reassuring her everything would be okay. Why wouldn't it be?

I'm sure Joy went to sleep before I did; she always did. I stayed up with Andrew Solomon's *Far from the Tree,* which I had been reading all summer, and did that night, until at least midnight, possibly later.

I can't remember anything specific or dramatic about the next morning, only being at the hospital, squeezing Joy's hand before she was led away to surgery, then settling into the waiting room. I don't remember what I did or what I read, so many of the mundane everyday things have been excised from my memory to make room for the awful ones.

When the surgery was finished we met up in recovery. Joy looked fine. Her doctor (whom I had not met before) breezed in for a minute, didn't say much, and seemed in a hurry to go. He had the cocky arrogance of an aging jock, and I didn't like him. I helped Joy dress and we took a cab home. We had already rented the prescribed ice machine (from the same doctor's office) that encased her leg under a thick canvas wrap that bulged and bloated with icy water pumped through the machine.

The rest of the day was normal other than the fact that Joy was mostly on the couch, leg up, ice machine doing its thing. She walked to and from the bathroom, from bedroom to living room, a good distance in the Flower Market loft we'd bought together more than thirty years ago, and she did this many times because she'd been told to walk.

For a while, nothing seemed out of the ordinary.

2
911

It is late morning of the following day. Joy is on the living room couch and has been all morning, reading *Wolf Hall,* or going over notes for *Food City,* the epic book on the history of New York food she is writing, when she complains of her leg feeling "odd and twitchy" and I notice that her face is flushed. I put my hand against her cheek. She feels warm. I ask her if she thinks she has a fever and she says she isn't sure but doesn't feel "quite right." I suggest she call the doctor, and she does. She tells the nurse or receptionist her symptoms — flushed face, possible fever, odd twitchy feeling in her leg — and says that she is feeling "congested," having some difficulty breathing. There is some conversation back and forth, no more than a couple of minutes, if that. When she hangs up, she says she's been told to wait until her follow-up appointment on Tuesday.

It is a Friday in mid-August.

"That's a long time to wait," I say, and ask again if she feels okay. She says not really, but the doctor's office does not appear worried, so she isn't either.

"No one wants to be bothered on a summer weekend," I say.

I have a few errands to run, some food, computer paper, more ice for the machine. I tell Joy I will be back in an hour, and I am. Joy is still on the couch, reading. I refill the ice machine. Her leg, she says, is feeling "very twitchy."

I suggest we take the ice pack off and have a look, but she doesn't think it's a good idea.

Do we talk about anything else? Dinner, I think. But I can't remember. After more than forty years of marriage we communicate without a lot of talk.

When we were first together we talked nonstop.

We'd met as undergrad art students at Boston University. I was a painting major; Joy, the more practical one, studying art education. A blind date neither one of us wanted — a friend of hers knew a friend of mine. I remember going to pick her up at her dorm, watching her come out of the elevator and walk toward me in her beige mini-jumper, dark tights that showed off

17

her legs, waist-long auburn hair, adorable pug nose and freckles. *Irish,* I thought (though it turned out she was Jewish). On the MTA trolley we talked easily and she smiled a lot and I noticed her perfect teeth (braces, I later learned), then her beautiful hands, long tapered fingers and surprisingly long nails, unlike other art school girls whose nails were usually cut short and crusted with paint, like mine.

I am in my studio at the back of the loft, too far away to hear if Joy calls — down a long hallway, past the kitchen, two bedrooms, two bathrooms, and Joy's office, plus my studio walls are soundproof — but she has her cell phone in case she needs me, and I can be by her side in less than a minute.

In the studio, I get to work on a book I have been trying to finish about a cop who loses his family in a random shooting, a novel with a loose association to *Crime and Punishment,* which I had recently reread, and had become obsessed with. My novel was unresolved, though Joy, always my first and best reader, liked it, and encouraged me to keep going. I remember thinking that I had gotten something wrong, something very basic to the story, that the villain, a hit man at the end of his days, should be the stand-in for Raskolnikov, not my hero cop, which is the way I had written it. It seemed like a revelation and I made notes on how I might rewrite it.

Normally, Joy would be right next door in her office, also soundproof, though we shared a wall. We had been working at home together for the past decade. Though there were times I found the togetherness a bit much, there was comfort in it too, like having an artist's colony of two. In grandiose moments I could imagine we were Dashiell Hammett and Lillian Hellman or Joan Didion and John Gregory Dunne.

My Raskolnikov notes did not take long. I couldn't have been in my studio for more than a half hour before going back to check on Joy, though she had not called.

Halfway down the hall I see her face is pale and she is reaching out to me. In my head I hear her say, *Where have you been?* but I don't think she says anything, her ability to speak already reduced to a croak, her eyes wide with a look I have never seen before: something between terror and pleading. I rush to her side and get my arms around her. She is gasping for breath and I tell her to breathe slowly as I fumble with my cell phone — or was it hers?

From the time I speak to the 911 operator until the firemen and paramedics arrive seems like hours though it is only a matter of minutes. The whole time I'm cradling Joy in my arms, telling her to breathe slowly, her eyes open wide and she grips my hand tightly as I repeat, "Hold on."

Then there are sirens outside and the buzzer is sounding, but how do I answer the bell? I can't move her, can't leave her, her breathing is labored — the buzzer is shrieking — I'm talking to her, *relax, breathe, relax, breathe,* but how to take the ten, twelve necessary steps to the elevator, to press the button to let the firemen in, but then I'm doing it, leaning Joy upright against the couch, her head lolls to the side and I try to right her but can't, the buzzer is shrieking again and I'm up now, sprinting across the room, pressing the buzzer that releases the building's front door, and I see them in the security camera — firemen in full gear — in the lobby, then crowding into the elevator, and when I hear the elevator engage I dash back to Joy, who is close to tumbling over and I am just getting my arms around her, gently pulling her toward me, when the elevator doors open and the firemen burst into the room.

3
INVISIBLE MAN

Everything is moving fast, firemen and paramedics in overdrive. Someone has tugged me away, my heart beating wildly, head light as if filled with helium, and I watch, a helpless man observing from the sidelines, though I see it in detail, every second of it becoming etched in my mind's eye, an endless movie loop, which later will become readily accessible at the flip of a synaptic switch, never something I do voluntarily but always with me and playing too often.

There is little talk other than the directions spoken quietly but urgently from one paramedic to another, over and under the pounding thoughts in my head: *This can't be happening — they are saving her — they are losing her — she will be okay — she is dying.*

I cannot say how long any of this goes on. The action is only a few feet in front of me, yet distant and far away as if I am watching through the wrong end of a telescope, in high definition one moment, blurred and indistinct the next, intensely real and unreal, all of it spiraling out of control just beyond my reach. My body is tingling though disconnected; I can't locate any feelings other than helplessness and panic, though I am trying hard not to show it, to act normal. Several times I ask what I can do, how I can help, but if there are any answers I no longer remember them.

I am the invisible man, there and not there.

The first paramedic team is replaced by a second, a woman, who seems more like a doctor, the others following her lead like Kabuki stagehands, in silence.

Finally, someone asks me a question: Is there another elevator, because the stretcher will not fit into the passenger elevator. I tell them there is a freight elevator and they ask me to get it and I am thankful to do something. I race down the stairs, six flights to the basement, then into the freight elevator, a dark, old device from the 1920s, where I flip the on switch and check the connections, things I have done countless times in the thirty years I have lived in the building, but cannot get it to work. Over and over I

22

am flipping switches and checking contacts, sweating and cursing and crying without knowing it until I taste tears on my lips. After a dozen more frantic attempts I give up and race up the basement stairs, cursing the machine and myself.

In the lobby, a neighbor I hardly know, a fairly new tenant, asks what's going on. There are fire engines and an ambulance in front of the building, their beacons streaking beams of startling red light through the glass doors and across the lobby, and the firemen have stopped the passenger elevator on my floor, so no one can use it. I can't imagine what I look like or how I am acting, but I must say something that makes sense, something about my wife being ill and that I can't get the freight elevator to work, before I race back up the five flights to tell the firemen and paramedics that the freight elevator isn't working at precisely the moment the new neighbor brings it to a stop on my floor.

Back in the loft I take in the scene as if for the first time: a swarm of paramedics and firemen in the living room and my wife on the floor, oxygen mask over her face. They lift her onto a gurney, which they carry into the stairwell, then into the freight elevator. I follow the other firemen and paramedics, all of us crowded into the passenger elevator, no one speaking, walkie-talkie devices chirping.

Outside, the world has gone surreal, the streets and buildings, stores and pedestrians dissolving, everything a vague painted backdrop behind the high-definition foreground action — my wife, unconscious on a stretcher, ambulance doors opening, paramedics lifting her in. I can't say if the day is hot or cool, if the sky is clear or cloudy. Street noise alternates between distant and deafening, sirens far away and muted one minute, shrieking the next. I try to get into the ambulance. I think I am shouting that I must stay with my wife when someone stops me and explains that it's more important for the emergency crew to be with her, once again the superfluous man.

I stand in the middle of the street, watching myself: lost, shrinking, weightless, and porous, as if I could blow away. Then someone has me by the shoulders and directs me into a car with the fire chief. I think it's the fire chief; I'm still not sure. So many factual details are gone while so many others are etched, sharp and clear.

I sit beside him, a man with a grim, determined face that I could draw from memory, and see the ambulance in front of us, filling the windshield like an oversized video game, lights flashing, siren blaring as we speed through the city, going the wrong way down one-way streets, buildings blurring, everything gray, color leached as if sucked away by our speed, feeling as though I am floating somewhere above the scene while I grip my seat so hard my fingers ache, none of it real, yet intensely, horrifically real, even while I continue telling myself: *This can't be happening — you are dreaming — you are going mad.*

The car radio crackles to life with static chatter and I am startled into the moment. I need to say something, to ask a question, but my mouth won't work. I swallow; it feels as if there is glass in my throat. I open my mouth but no words come out. I try again. *You know how to do this.* I take a couple of quick shallow breaths and manage a sentence, "Just — tell me — she is — going — to be — all right." After a long moment the fire chief says, "They're doing all they can," the whole time staring straight ahead, his voice uninflected, never once taking his eyes off the road. It is a canned response, one I will hear again.

The car bumps over potholes and careens around corners to keep pace with the speeding ambulance before we come to a jolting stop at the hospital, where I bound out of the car and follow the gurney, practically running beside it, trying to hold on until I am tugged away, by whom I have no idea.

I catch a last glimpse of my wife on the stretcher, inert and pale, disappearing into the emergency room, all of this in split seconds, like frames of a silent movie before the emergency room doors slam shut.

4
WAITING

The waiting room is small, no more than six or eight feet wide by ten or twelve feet long. There is a two-seater sofa against one wall, a couple of plastic upholstered chairs against another, no windows. I am alone, my body tingling as if I have grabbed hold of an electric wire, my mind a fractured kaleidoscope of thoughts, one toppling over another, fragmented — pictures of Joy on the couch, the floor, the stretcher, the race to get here — slipping and sliding over one another.

I suck in a deep breath and stare at a television tucked high into a corner. I can't tell if the sound is on or off, my brain buzzing so loud with words and half sentences. Something that feels important nags at the corner of my mind, but I can't get at it.

I steady myself against the chair. For a moment I think I might faint. And then I am back in time, freshman year of art school, Thanksgiving break, at home, in my bedroom, cutting a mat for a drawing and slicing my hand with an X-Acto knife, blood everywhere, rushing upstairs and my father pouring peroxide over the cut and the walls starting to spin, then slow, and his voice slowing too, before everything goes black. I awake in my father's arms, a rarity. We were not close. Another memory slips in through a crack in my mind: my father's funeral. I see his face transformed into a mask by the mortician's makeup, then a dozen other thoughts about my father come rushing at me — working summers at his Manhattan dress company, meeting famous and semi-famous clients — former Miss America Bess Myerson, the only Jewish Miss America, whom my mother revered, the actress Polly Bergen, Marilyn Monroe, an incandescent memory — along with a contrasting image of my father's partner's wife, an anorexic gorgon, whom my mother blamed for my father's heart attack. I see my sister in the knotty pine den of our Long Island home, me beside her, both of us pretending to watch television and waiting for news of whether or not our father will die. I am fourteen, my sister almost three years older and on the edge of hysteria. I am already playing the caretaker, telling her *everything will be okay.*

I have not fainted. I lay a hand on one of the waiting room's chairs to steady myself.

I feel ashamed. I am usually in control, or pretend to be, the one to tell my family everything will be fine. I sag into the chair and take deep breaths. The air smells of pine cleaner over the sick sour smell of hospital. I close my eyes and a sentence unfurls in my mind like a banner or skywriting: *Would you really want me to be miserable?*

It takes a second to locate the forty-year-old memory — Joy and I first married, a salesman calling to offer me a deal on life insurance. I said, *No thanks.* A few days later, a follow-up letter, urging me to think about my future, about taking care of my wife in the event that I died. I ignored it. A week later he called again.

Look, I said, *I am only twenty-two years old. If I die, I do not want my wife to get anything. Understand? I want her to be miserable!*

He never called back.

I thought this was funny and repeated it to Joy, who laughed, then said: *Would you really want me to be miserable?*

I stare at the waiting room walls and see us in that Park Slope, Brooklyn, apartment, our first, the second floor of a brownstone

29

— pressed-tin ceilings, dark wood floors, a fireplace — beautiful and cheap, the neighborhood still rough, long before Brooklyn gentrified. Joy and I often joked that we lived in places before they were chic — Park Slope, Hoboken, Manhattan's West Twenties — that they only became desirable once we left. Pictures tumble through my mind: the painting studio I created in the dining alcove of our Park Slope apartment; Pablo's Towing Station with its guard dogs and barbed-wire fence just beside our two-story factory building in Hoboken; getting mugged at knifepoint on Sixth Avenue a week after moving into our Twenty-Eighth Street loft.

I see Joy with her long red hair, me with my muttonchops and serious porn star mustache, twenty-somethings playing at being adults, though we never really felt it.

I feel like a boy, I said one day, and before I could say another word, Joy said, *Men are always boys,* and that it is exactly how I feel as I sit in this hospital waiting room, like a boy, the way I'd felt at Jones Beach when I was six or seven and got lost and the lifeguards took care of me and gave me ice cream, not an entirely unpleasant memory — I remember liking the ice cream and the lifeguards' attention — but there is no lifeguard here.

The word *life guard* separates and vibrates in my mind with urgent new meaning.

I am startled out of my memory by a young woman, African American and pretty, clipboard under her arm, standing beside me. She starts asking questions: my wife's name, Social Security number, our insurance, and I ask one back, "She's going to be okay, isn't she?"

She touches my arm gently and says, "They're doing what they can."

It is the same thing the fire chief said, but I hear the slight modification.

My mantra starts up, *everything will be okay, everything will be okay, everything will be okay,* so loud in my head that I have to ask her to repeat everything she says.

Then she is gone and I am alone again. I pace back and forth across the small room, then have that teasing thought, something I am trying to remember, but whatever it is I have tucked away and locked so tightly I cannot get at it, though it continues to gnaw at the borders of my brain like a rat trying to gain entry, but I refuse to let it in.

Instead, a recent fight Joy and I had about her book slides into whatever fissure that gnawing rat has created: how I said she needed to cut a chapter and how she took my criticism as an attack.

You don't think I'm a good writer.

I never said that.

But it's clear.

I'm thinking I shouldn't help her at all, that she's too defensive about her writing, at the same time worrying that she may be too sick to work when she gets home. I imagine calling her editor, what I will say and how I will make it okay, because it's what I always try to do: make things okay, even when I can't, even knowing Joy would never allow me to call her editor, to be *The Husband.*

I know our friends see Joy as the level-headed one and me as the more erratic, more "artistic" and temperamental, and there is some truth in that, though beneath Joy's cool demeanor is someone who is not always so in control — terrified of heights, anxious about traveling, obsessive about schedules, a worrier — and I think I am pretty much the only one who knows that. I also know that Joy can be incredibly stubborn in good ways and bad, and how that stubbornness enabled her to change her life, to go back to school for a master's in food studies, to become a food historian, recognized in her field, and how she must get home to finish her book, which will bring her the attention and admiration she deserves. And I'm sure she will.

Then I am not so sure.

5
PREMONITIONS

I don't want to have the surgery.
Why not?
Because I think I'm going to die.
Don't be silly.
A conversation from a few days earlier.
A premonition?
I do not believe in such things. And neither did Joy, though she said it not only to me but to our daughter, who also dismissed the idea.
Something we both regret.
But isn't that what one says, *Don't be silly, you'll be fine,* especially when it's routine, non-life-threatening outpatient surgery?
Because I think I'm going to die.
A shiver racks my body and I try to bat the sentence away. It's absurd. Even now. With all that has happened. No way she is going to die. They are taking care of her, all of those doctors and nurses in the emergency room just next door.

Because I think I'm going to die.

I see my father's face in death.

I see my mother-in-law in the hospital just before dying.

I see my mother sitting shiva for her brother, her father, then her mother, who had come to live with us after my grandfather died, and who I found in bed, on her side, turned toward the wall. That morning she had placed a photo of herself beside ones of her dead husband and son. My mother noticed and asked why. My grandmother said, "Because I belong with them."

A premonition, or had she willed it?

I see myself going downstairs and saying to my mother, *I think Grandma is dead.* I am thirteen years old and have come home from school in the middle of the day after faking being sick to get out of gym, and my mother has picked me up. We have just gotten back to our suburban split-level home and I've been sent upstairs to ask my grandmother what she wants for lunch, and I will forever think that by feigning illness, by making my mother leave her mother, that I am responsible for my grandmother's death, though she had been ill and failing for weeks.

I suddenly think: I have to call my daughter.

I fumble the cell phone from my pocket. It drops out of my hand and hits the floor. When I retrieve it, there is a diagonal crack from one end of the screen to the other. It feels like another premonition, significant, as if something has been divided — time, my life.

My daughter's number is on speed dial, a good thing; I would not have been able to remember it. I say, *Mom is sick, please get here right away,* or something close to that. Days later, Dorie will tell me that she knew it was bad because she had never heard that tone in my voice.

I go into the hall and pace. I replace the image of Joy gasping for breath with that picture of her in the beige jumper and her waist-long auburn hair — and now an entire loop of old memories starts to unfurl as if they are things I need to hold on to and preserve: our wedding, so long ago and faraway, the bride and groom beautiful young strangers, the flowers in Joy's hair, which we found later, wilted or dying, and how we laughed as I tugged them out; our daughter, moments after being born, in Joy's arms, tiny and perfect, her first bath in our kitchen sink, her first laugh at six months, thrilling and unforgettable, then at twelve or thirteen, visiting day at summer camp, her naturally dirty blond hair a startling platinum and she is swearing, *I didn't do anything to it,* which leads to a trivial conversation just a week ago, Joy saying to our artist friend Jane Kent, who has let her hair go gray, that no woman should ever go gray (and Joy didn't), which leads me to Joy's constant worry (no, obsession) about her weight and how she will undoubtedly lose a few pounds from this ordeal and be pleased, which leads me to thinking how Joy always buys a sweater after a successful breast checkup as a kind of good luck charm against the breast cancer that killed her mother and how she will surely buy one after this, which leads me to her mother arriving at our loft when Dorie was born, and I had come home from the hospital to take a shower after Joy's sixteen hours of labor and how, when I buzzed her into the building, I singsonged into the intercom, "Come in, *Grandma,*" and later, the nurse at the hospital saying, "Wait till you smell her," referring to our baby girl, who smelled "like roses" Joy said, and it was true; for days we sniffed her as if she were an exotic flower.

My mind is a shortwave radio, snatching thoughts from the ether of my life.

Our second or third date, three movies in one day, first Boston University's art theater for a Luis Buñuel double feature, *Viridiana* and *The Exterminating Angel.* Afterward, in a diner on Commonwealth Avenue, Joy and I dissecting and deconstructing the movies, talking about film and art school and what we wanted out of life, no idea that our lives would include each other. Then, deciding we needed an antidote to those dark Buñuel films, going to see *The Umbrellas of Cherbourg,* in downtown Boston, Joy sobbing at the end, and that memory segues into six months after Dorie was born, and Joy telling the actor Warren Beatty, whom we were meeting for the first time through a friend, how, in junior high school, she'd seen *Splendor in the Grass* three times, each time crying herself sick. I add, "It's true!" Warren says, "You knew each other in high school?" I say, "No, it was in college, at a drive-in outside of Boston, and Joy cried all over again." I graze fingertips over my black eye and the bandage that covers half of my cheek (two days earlier, deciding it was the moment I absolutely had to install stereo speakers in the high ceiling corners of my studio despite sleep deprivation from the baby and Joy advising against it, I had fallen off the ladder and stabbed my cheek with scissors requiring several stitches). "I don't always look like this," I say. Warren says,

"That's good," and scoops up a mouthful of Chinese takeout. Later that night, he held our baby girl and cooed at her, promising to take care of her forever (which he didn't), and when we got home Joy said with a huff, "I have to meet Warren Beatty *now,* when I'm somebody's *mother,* when I'm *fat!*" and even here it brings a smile to my face.

Little pieces of our life race through my mind, how I often say with a touch of irony, *Joy is a food historian who loves to eat but not cook,* or *How did I manage to find the only food historian who doesn't like to cook?* and then I'm thinking about her book, her life's work, and the phrase *life's work* triggers a sick sinking feeling that starts to uncoil inside me and I grasp at anything concrete — do I need to get Joy a change of clothes, did I take my house keys, which I can't find in any of my pockets — anything at all to forget that I am a helpless husband in a hospital emergency room waiting to hear if my wife will live or die.

I stare at the television. The blur and flash of images make me think, *Things are normal, Joy is going to be fine,* and I shake my head up and down as if to confirm this to anyone who may be watching, though I am alone in this ugly, airless room that I will never forget.

An absurd thought: *Was Joy wearing ear-rings?* I make a mental note to make sure they are not lost and I see the two of us twenty years ago in a Victorian jewelry flea market, three hours outside of London where Joy spent all of our cash so that I had to bribe a taxi driver to take us back to London via a stop at American Express. And later, Joy laying out the jewelry for her British friend, who says, "You like this kind of stuff? It's so *old,*" and the look on Joy's face, a mix of surprise and disappointment followed by laughter that I want to hang on to, but it's already been exchanged for the look of terror on her face when I walked into our living room, which was . . . how long ago?

I check my watch. No matter how many times I look I can't keep track of the time. Still, I think it must be a good sign that this is taking so long — though I do not believe in signs.

Because I think I'm going to die.

I look at my watch again.

I walk in and out of the room. I pace up and down the hall, a tunnel of blue-white fluorescent glare.

Everything will be okay.

I turn the sentence over in my mind, mas-sage and polish it until it feels like something physical I can hold in my hand.

I remind myself that Joy is a healthy person who eats carefully and exercises daily, how she criticizes the way I eat and how it annoys her that I live on cookies but never get fat. I think about the way she freezes me out after we fight and I sleep in the living room or the guest room or in my studio and how I fume and how she fumes, and how we do not abide by the slogan *never go to bed angry;* we have often gone to bed *seething.* I make a deal with God: if He makes Joy well I promise we will never fight again. I see Joy and me on our way back from Rome, on a plane caught in a storm, terrifying thunder and lightning outside the windows, the plane knocked about like a soccer ball, and how I'd made a silent bargain with God that if He got us through the flight I'd never fly again, but since I have flown dozens and dozens of times since then I wonder if the God I do not believe in will believe me — and why should He?

I am making these promises to myself and to God when the waiting room door opens and my daughter comes in, her beautiful face pinched with anxiety, and I hug her to me and she asks in a small scared voice, "What *happened?*"

41

I do not give her details, just that Joy got very ill. I say, *They're working on Mom now and she will be okay,* trying hard to believe it because as I say it there is another voice inside my head that is saying the opposite.

We start the waiting process together. We talk. We hold hands. We stand. We sit. I can't say how much time goes by, though now I have my twenty-nine-year-old daughter by my side, both comforting and a burden. I look at her and think: I am no longer a helpless husband waiting to hear if my wife will live or die, I am also a helpless father.

And then the waiting room door opens and a doctor comes in.

6
WE MAY NEVER KNOW

The doctor's face is sober, his eyes dark, and I know before he speaks, before he says, "We did all we could," and my daughter screams *"NO!"* so loud it cuts through me, the worst sound I have ever heard, and she is already crying so hard and I hold her against my chest and she sobs into me while the doctor, who has a soft, kind way about him, tells me that they tried everything to revive my wife but failed, and that it is probably for the best because her brain had been deprived of oxygen for too long, and I force myself to listen, to make sense of what he is saying, nodding, consciously trying to act normal, thinking, *This isn't happening,* my arm around my daughter, whose cries vibrate through me like electric shocks and bring tears to my eyes, though I have gone numb. I thank the doctor — the man who just told me that my wife has died — because it's what I have been brought up to do no matter what I am feeling, though I have no idea what I am feeling other than the excruciating pain of my daughter, who is shuddering against me with deep convulsive sobs.

Then I am in the hallway feeling as if I've been shot through with Novocain, standing with the doctor, asking what happened. He says he's not sure, and adds: *We may never know.*

My brain is shrieking: *What do you mean we may never know?* But I say nothing. I can barely feel anything, let alone understand what he is saying. It is the beginning of a medical mystery but I don't know that yet.

He asks if I will authorize an autopsy and I say yes, and he tells me I made the right decision, and I nod as if he's given me some sort of compliment, and he tells me he will be performing the autopsy himself and that I can contact him the next day for the results, and he gives me his card, lays a hand on my shoulder, says he's sorry, and then he is gone.

I stand in the hall, not knowing what to do or how long I stand there. I feel something inside me collapsing. Then I am back in the waiting room, arms around my daughter, her head buried in the crook of my shoulder, my neck wet with her tears.

Less than a minute later, a hospital social worker interrupts us. There are forms to be filled out, personal articles to be claimed. I despise him, not only because he has interrupted us or that he is there at the worst moment in our lives, but because he is cold and officious and just plain creepy. I want to say, *How the hell did you get this job?* but I follow him down the hall to his office.

Do I fill out forms? I can't remember.

I say to Dorie, "I have to call Aunt Kathy."

I don't remember what I said to my wife's older sister. What I remember is going out to meet her and seeing her with her husband as they came rushing into the hospital and I will never forget her face, red and ruined by tears, the two of us falling into each other and her crying "Oh my God! What *happened*?"

She wants to see Joy's body, something I have already refused, but I go with her out of obligation or guilt — *if Kathy can take it, so can I* — a mistake I will forever regret, seeing my wife like that, bruised and inert as I stand there watching the brave big sister lovingly stroke her little sister's face and saying good-bye, tears streaming down her face, and me, one more time, pinned against a wall trying not to see it.

I don't know how long we stay there, but at some point we are walking down the hospital corridor, two shocked and wounded soldiers, leaning against each other for support.

Back in the waiting room, my daughter and I are locked in an embrace and I am trying to console her while struggling to control and contain my emotions, both of us sick with grief that has only just begun.

■ ■ ■ ■

PART II
AFTER

■ ■ ■ ■

Part II
After

7
LEAVING AND ARRIVING

I don't remember leaving the hospital, or getting the bags — one with Joy's watch and jewelry and one with her shoes — but they are in my hands.

I don't remember the cab ride home.

I come into the living room and see it in disarray, dining room table askew, coffee table at an angle far away from the couch, books on the floor along with medical wrappers and papers left behind by the paramedics, everything in glaring specificity. I crab-walk across the floor scooping up papers and wrappers, trying hard not to look at them. I push furniture back into place.

Did Dorie come home with me? I can't say, but she is with me now, along with her husband, Drew.

Did my sister-in-law, Kathy, and brother-in-law, Charlie, follow in their car? I have no idea but they are here as well.

I am bleeding through time and space.

For a while I sit with Kathy and Charlie and Dorie and Drew and we talk, but about what I can't tell you.

I keep glancing at Kathy, then away. She looks so much like Joy with her red hair and freckles, it is both reassuring and painful. I have known Kathy almost as long as Joy, and I love her. She is smart and kind, with an easy smile, though she is not smiling now. I can't help but think of the two sisters, together since Joy's birth, suddenly separated, but I don't believe it. I keep waiting for Joy to make an entrance, for someone to wake me from this nightmare, the first of several clichés that will become reality.

Dorie and Drew sit close together. Drew's arm is around Dorie's shoulder and I wonder if it is awkward for them — they have been separated for months, a beautiful young couple who have uncoupled in a year's time.

Here's what I know:

At some point, Kathy and Charlie leave.

Dorie and Drew go to sleep in the guest room.

I take a sleeping pill but lie in bed, awake.

In the middle of the night I turn on the television but have no idea what I watch.

I go to the bathroom.

I go into the kitchen and get something to drink.

I sit in the living room, in the dark.

I try to be quiet so I will not wake Dorie and Drew. I am happy knowing they are here, to have their company, to not be alone, though I feel completely alone.

I have lived in this loft for thirty years, but it feels alien.

I stare into the dark.

For a moment I am back in the hospital waiting room, but when I shake my head to dislodge the picture it is as if I have simply rearranged the pixels because now it is another hospital's waiting room, part of an earlier rush of memory — our first date — Joy and I arriving at a party just as my roommate, John, has gotten into a fistfight with uninvited townies, beaten up while people yell and scream over blasting music, the Rolling Stones' "(I Can't Get No) Satisfaction," a few of us trying to break it up, the townies shouting, "He started it!" and I'm sure they're right, John can be a nasty drunk.

Then we are in a Boston hospital, John's girlfriend, Claudia, the one who has arranged this careering-toward-disaster blind date, and Joy, who has offered to come along over my protests and apologies, all of us huddled around John in an emergency room cubicle, John sitting up now making jokes.

I watch Joy out of the corner of my eye, take in the curves of her body under the tight beige jumper, so unlike the girls I have dated or been with in the past, not my usual "type," which is dark-haired and overtly sexy. Joy is fair and freckled, quiet and sweet, patting John's arm and chatting with Claudia to put them at ease, already the sensible girl I will get to know later. "Some date," I whisper, and she offers an ironic smile. Later, when I take her home and say it again, she says, "I've had worse," laughs and kisses my cheek and tells me to take care of John, and I watch her disappear into her dormitory, her long red hair swaying back and forth like some TV ad for shampoo, romantic and soft focus.

I am startled back into the moment by a shrieking siren and red lights going off like firecrackers in the large dark windows of my living room, and the events of the day start to play as if someone has thrown a switch.

I go back to bed but cannot close my eyes. When I do, variations of the same images tear across my brain — the look of terror on Joy's face, the paramedics trying to revive her, big sister stroking little sister's cheek — all of it accompanied by a hollow, echoing silence, as though I am in the eye of a hurricane or adrift in outer space.

I stare at the ceiling and the thought I have been trying to remember while I rode with the fire chief and sat in the emergency waiting room starts to uncoil and I can almost see it — something that happened just before or after the paramedics arrived — but when I try to hold on, it disappears.

Then it's morning and I am writing Joy's obituary.

Kathy is there. So are Dorie and Drew.

My good friend Jane O'Keefe, whom I had asked to call our friends to tell them the terrible news — which she did, and I still don't know how — now calls the obit into the *Times*. I have known Jane since graduate school at Pratt, where we had adjoining painting studios, and we have been friends ever since. When Joy and I married, she and Jane became instant friends though they were polar opposites, Jane tall and brash, Joy petite and quiet.

Now Jane suggests I plan some sort of memorial because there will be no funeral, but I can't remember if she is actually there, in person, or if we discuss this on the phone.

I know she's there later, but I can't reconstruct the order of events.

A part of me is functioning — walking, talking, doing what's necessary — my brain simply remembering what its former functions were, but no longer connected.

I call my friend Judd and tell him what's happened. He says, "I'm coming over." I tell him no, that I'm okay, but twenty minutes later he's there and we sit in my studio for hours, just the two of us, and though I can't remember what we talk about it is incredibly comforting to have him there.

I should have learned from this — that I needed comfort though I said I did not. It was to become a motif, a stance I maintained for months, the strong man who needs no one.

Do women do this, push people away, or is it easier for them to ask for help? Is it similar to the way men don't ask for directions, as if we should always know where we are going, or simply never get lost? In a way, it's funny, though at this particular moment in my life it was not, because I was so lost and needed help but could not ask for it.

Friends like Judd didn't listen to my proclamations of well-being. He knew better, and was there for me. My friend and neighbor Ben, an artist almost half my age, surprised me with his wise-beyond-years kindness, coming upstairs at midnight or two in the morning to keep me company, a bottle of whiskey tucked under his arm. Two examples of "sensitive" men, though we didn't talk about feelings — they were simply *there*.

Other friends were there too. Others stayed away. Still others offered outrageous balms and provocative alternatives to grief. Some of these are well worth relating for their entertainment or shock value, and I will.

But not yet, because it is the morning after my wife has died and I am a sleepwalker, hung over from meds and searching for the emergency room doctor's card, which I can't find but I know has to be here, some-where.

8
THE BEGINNING OF A
MEDICAL MYSTERY

The doctor's card is not in my pockets, my wallet, nor the mess on my bedside table.

Did I imagine him giving it to me?

I hear Joy in my mind: *You lose everything.*

And it's true. I do.

I also hear her consoling me: *It will turn up.*

Dorie is standing in the kitchen, coffee mug to her lips, blond hair in disarray, blue-gray eyes puffy and bruised looking. The way she stands, elbows pressed against her sides, suggests she is literally holding herself together. I am about to ask how she is doing, but stop. How *can* she be doing? I don't want to ask her about the doctor — the man who broke the news of her mother's death, a wound inflicted less than twenty-four hours ago — but I do.

She shakes her head; she does not recall seeing him give me his card.

Am I crazy?

I close my eyes. I see the doctor's card in

my hand, then tucking it into my breast pocket.

In my bedroom I find last night's shirt crumpled on top of the wicker hamper. There is nothing in the pocket. I look inside the hamper and under it, then dump its contents onto the floor, rustle through underwear and socks, hold T-shirts up and shake them out.

No card.

I sit there a minute, no longer sure why I am on my bedroom floor sorting through dirty laundry. My mind has lost the thread.

Then I remember.

I call the hospital but no one seems to know the doctor's name. I am transferred from one department to another, but no one can help and I soon give up; I simply can't deal with it. It casts a feeling of unreality over an event that is already unreal, as if I made it up or dreamt it.

Am I dreaming now?

I sit on my bed and touch it, then the walls, then my legs, to make sure I am awake. But isn't this the sort of thing one does in a dream? I *could* be dreaming. I'm really not sure.

A few days later I find the doctor's last name scribbled on a piece of paper in my handwriting.

I call the hospital again, but no one knows who he is or how I can reach him.

How is that possible? I ask.

We have many emergency room doctors, a woman tells me.

But I have his name. Surely there must be a way —

She transfers me to someone else, one more person who has no idea who this doctor is.

How is it that no one in the hospital knows this doctor or how I can reach him?

I am told to call the county coroner's office and I do. There is no record of my wife having had an autopsy. They tell me to check back with the hospital. But by then my head is spinning and my energy has waned, so I let it go.

A mistake. Perhaps if I had pursued the doctor's identity further, and right away, it might have made a difference, but just then, a day after my wife has died, I was incapable of even one more phone call.

These are the kinds of details that Joy would have hunted down, the researcher in her refusing to give up until she got answers. But not me.

During the weeks that followed, weeks of shock and grief, of endless days that bled into sleepless nights, this was a theme: I could not act, I could not ask for help, I did none of the things that one is supposed to do. I neglected to obtain the necessary legal papers that would authorize me as the beneficiary of my wife's estate and so the hospital would not release the autopsy results, which will take close to two years of battling the surrogate court to get. But this is another, longer story about trying to find out what really happened, incredibly frustrating and ultimately shocking.

For now, it is enough to say that the once cool, in-control husband became so helpless and muddled that he lost the attending physician's card and could not fill out the necessary forms to become the legal guardian of his dead wife's estate.

I have heard women, widows, complain of husbands who kept them in the dark about money or legal matters so that when their husbands died they were stunned and helpless. Here I was, the husband, the *widower,* who had lost a wife, and though my wife did not keep me in the dark, I became as helpless as any *widow.*

I stare at the contents of my bedside table drawer, which I have dumped onto the bed — collar stays, orphaned buttons, loose change, scraps of paper — then the heap of dirty laundry on the floor, and I wonder if it is even worse because I am a man, because our culture says that men are supposed to take charge and be in control? But I *was* in control, holding my feelings in, not asking anyone for help, busy constructing and wearing my mask of normality, all of which took so much effort it made it impossible for me to do anything else.

And for that, I will pay a price.

9
UNMOORED

We all think we know what grief is going to be like. We know the clichés about losing a loved one — shock, sadness, loneliness, to name the obvious — and they are all true. But it's not until we actually lose someone that we experience it from the inside, that the clichés have any meaning.

Grief was not like anything I had imagined.

Mine came in waves of exhaustion. I would be walking down the street or up from the subway and think, *I just can't make it. I will have to stop and sit down on these filthy concrete steps.* My legs were like dead weights. I often felt as if I were trudging through half-set cement. For the first time in my life I felt old.

I had no energy, though I pushed myself to go out every night. I could not be alone in the loft, especially in the evening.

Everywhere I looked I saw my wife. I was

going to say, *Everywhere I looked I saw Joy,* but it struck me as ironic because I saw Joy everywhere, but did not see *joy* anywhere.

I flip-flopped between thinking the worst had happened, so nothing could affect me, and feeling the complete opposite: I was a weakened slob that *everything* affected too much.

The days were long — I felt raw and exposed, as if people could see through me and into me — the nights interminable.

There are images stored in my brain like half-developed negatives: myself in bed wide awake or wandering my loft in the middle of the night, of seeing friends and putting on a show of good humor, of waking up and longing to talk to my wife so together we could make sense of all this.

If asked for one word to describe how I felt those first days, weeks, months, even year, I'd have said *unmoored.*

I had lost my anchor. I was at sea, floating and floundering.

Grief's terrain was unfamiliar to me, rocky, perilous, and unstable. I never perceived nor felt any prescribed set of moods or stages to my grief, only unexpected moments of paralysis, sadness, or confusion. I slogged through the days as if in a dream where nothing connects.

I've taught writing for a number of years since publishing my first novel and have often given my crime-writing students an exercise: put a character into complete darkness with the thought that something bad has happened or is about to happen and make the reader *feel* it.

I no longer had to imagine it. It was as if I had stumbled into a black room and was trying to find my way out without a guide, and with only half of my senses.

My life had changed forever, though it had not yet registered. On the surface, things remained unchanged: my home was still there, so was the outside world — all the physical circumstances of my life appeared normal.

Joy was there too, her cosmetics in the bathroom, clothes in the closets, the pottery she collected, the furniture she chose, the book she was reading still on the glass-topped side table in the living room.

I lift the copy of *Wolf Hall* and note where Joy has turned down the page; she had only twenty pages to go.

In the bedroom, on her bedside table, a small porcelain dish, in it an antique silver neck chain. I hold it in my hand and think, *memento mori*, a term I first learned in art history class when we studied Christian art, crypt ornamentation, portraits of people holding skulls, and still lifes of dead rabbits — such obvious images of death they had a term for it, *nature morte.* Literally: dead nature.

I did what was necessary, what I needed to do, by rote, though my usual cognitive skills and defenses did not seem to be working. I was never sure if I was reading situations or people correctly, my reactions either too extreme or nothing at all.

The process of grieving was, for me, filled with self-doubt, my normal insecurities magnified, the best and worst close to the surface.

Am I doing a good job of grieving? was not a question I asked myself but was a free-floating sensation. It was difficult to know: Is this the way one is *supposed* to feel, or just *my* problem? An impossible question to answer because we are individuals with our own sets of problems and psychological makeup, though I think grief puts us all in the same lost-at-sea boat.

Past experiences with death came to me unexpectedly and in vivid detail. One, from when I was a teenager, began to haunt me.

My high school friend Linda had been ill and out of school for a while, though none of us knew the severity of her illness. I don't know what I expected when I went to visit her, nervous I would find a skeletal version of my buoyant smiling friend. She was in bed but upright, and looked the same — dark hair, olive complexion, light green eyes, an unusually pretty girl, smiling and chatty as ever, and we talked of school and things that were going on, nothing special. I visited a second time and she still seemed okay. I think we played cards. I remember she was so alive.

It wasn't long after that Linda was in the hospital and there was talk of transfusions. I knew this because my father was going to give blood, they had the same unusual type, my parents speaking in whispers, so that I knew it was bad, though still I was sure she'd be okay.

We got the news of her death at school, and what I remember most are her many girlfriends clinging to one another, sobbing and staggering through the corridors like drunkards, a display of emotion I couldn't, wouldn't, possibly allow or demonstrate. It was a stunning reality for those who knew her and had been her friend, to lose her, to lose one of *us,* sixteen years old, though I don't remember any of the boys crying.

Did the girls feel better because they did,

because they let out all of that sadness in a way the boys could not?

Not long ago, I met up with a high school friend who told me that Linda's mother had refused to see any of her daughter's girl-friends. It had seemed cruel to my friend back then, though she understood it now: the idea of seeing all of those young, open faces with their lives stretching in front of them.

This was the only person in my youth, someone my age, someone I knew, who had died, and it started to recur in my mind and dreams in a way that it hadn't ever before, though it was not my first experience with death.

My favorite uncle, one of my mom's five brothers, died when I was eleven. I was twelve when I lost my maternal grandfather, Sam Brill, the sweetest, kindest, funniest man I ever knew. In many ways, the most important man in my young life, who loved me unconditionally and defended me against my father. When he died I felt more alone than ever before, though I never talked about it, not to my mother, surely not to my father, who expressed no emotion about the loss, though I think he loved his father-in-law — everyone did. I don't remember my mother showing much emotion either, though I know she adored her father. My parents were a stoic pair, and obviously good teachers, or at least compelling examples.

I did not know how to mourn these past losses and still didn't, though I would have to learn. When it comes to loss we do not get a choice. It happens. One minute your partner, your loved one, is right there beside you, the next he or she is gone.

I don't believe any of us are prepared for this kind of personal loss and surely I was not, no warning, no major illness, no way to prepare for the impact, as if Joy and I had been driving and sideswiped by an out-of-control car and only I had survived the crash.

I could not stop thinking: If only we'd had time — a day, a week, even an hour — all the things I might have said. But there are no second chances to say good-bye, only chores to be done that offer little solace, and one of them had to be done now.

10
THE BODY

The body — *Joy's body* — needed to be picked up from the hospital by a funeral home right away. There it is, a hideous fact of death that cannot, could not, be avoided.

For this first job I enlisted my grown-up nephew, my sister's middle son, a sweet serious young man who appears to take care of his family in the way I always made mine laugh, something that has brought us close. He tells me now that he wanted to say no, that the idea terrified him, but he came through, and I couldn't have done it without him.

He did an Internet search and came up with a funeral home in the West Village. He says I gave him a list of questions to ask, something I no longer remember, but presumably he got the answers.

I'm not sure if we walked or took the subway. I only remember being there.

The place looks like a 1950s television set for a funeral home, something out of *The Addams Family:* heavy maroon drapes, dark wood, dim lighting, the smell of cedar and dust. Under any other circumstances I would be cracking jokes.

The young woman in charge seems out of place. She is pretty, brunette, and incredibly chipper. Too chipper. She speaks quickly, says something and smiles, says something else and smiles again. I can barely follow her. I want her to slow down, to be serious, to stop *smiling*! Is this what she's been taught in undertaker school — to be unnervingly cheery?

Here's what I remember:

Sitting at her large wooden desk.

Discussing cremation.

Writing out a check for a thousand dollars.

The young woman telling me it would be wise to order several death certificates because they will "come in handy." I think that costs extra.

There is talk about the ashes but I can't remember what. I am numb though working overtime to appear normal, my leitmotif for those days, weeks, and months: *act normal.*

I take in the surroundings and try to

believe they are real, not a stage set or a bad dream. A part of me wants to, needs to, believe, but a larger part does not. It's ironic that even here I can't believe it, that no one ever wants to accept death and yet we are all going to die. Is it just too terrifying to imagine?

I glance at an open catalog on the undertaker's desk, picture after picture of caskets, each more baroque than the last, and I think that no matter what people tell us about their near-death experiences — the glorious white light and the long-dead loved ones waiting to meet us on the other side — we know in our heart of hearts that we just don't know.

I manage to ask the young woman if she has heard anything about the autopsy.

She gives me a blank stare.

"You can't pick up the body if it hasn't been done, can you?" I ask.

"I'm sure everything is being done correctly," she says and smiles.

"Have you inquired? Have you spoken to anyone at the hospital?"

She shuffles papers on her desk and I am momentarily transfixed by her shiny red nail polish.

"I'm sure it's all in order," she says.

But is it?

I agree to the cremation. She tells me I can pick up the ashes in a few days.

Weeks later, my nephew and I are having dinner in a small Chelsea restaurant and he tells me he has something to "confess," something that has been bothering him. I can't imagine what, but he looks very somber. He is a serious young man but this is different; he cannot look me in the eye.

"What is it?" I ask.

He pauses a moment, his large brown eyes restless and uneasy, as if he wants to flee. "Remember the girl at the funeral home?"

I recall the way-too-cheery brunette, and nod.

"I called her."

"About what?"

"To see if she wanted to go out on a date."

This takes a few seconds to register. Then, I start laughing.

My nephew looks confused, then lets out a long breath. "I'm *so* glad you're laughing, Uncle Jonny. But how come?"

I am laughing at the realization that my very serious nephew had been flirting with the funeral home director while I was arranging my wife's cremation, the absurdity of it, which I had completely missed at the time.

I make some sort of sarcastic comment about picking up girls at funeral homes and he looks embarrassed and crestfallen, until I tell him I am kidding, that it is one of the few laughs I've had in a long while, that it is perfectly fine.

He lets out another deep breath, then goes on to explain how she is his type, Italian and Jewish.

I wonder how he knows this and he explains that he asked.

He also tells me that she has a boyfriend but it's nothing serious, and that she is going on vacation and he will call her again when she gets back — he talks very fast, practically breathless as he explains — apparently their phone call has been somewhat extensive.

For a moment I imagine they will date, get engaged, marry, and that he will have this absurd story for the rest of his life: *We met when my aunt died and I accompanied my uncle to the funeral parlor. It was either when he was signing the papers so the funeral home could pick up my aunt's body, or while he was signing for the cremation, that I looked up and locked eyes with* — Terri? Angie? Susie? — *that we fell in love.*

But the date never happens, or it doesn't work out. Maybe for the best.

Still, it's proof to me that life goes on, the idea that my nephew could be flirting at such a time — I couldn't help but see the humor in it.

It's strange that this is now my strongest association and memory of that awful visit to the funeral home and I have my nephew to thank for it. He was there for me in a terrible time. So what if he had sex on the brain?

What I wanted that day, and so many others, was to tell Joy about it — the *Addams Family* funeral home, the undertaker, our nephew's big flirt. I didn't even have to make it funny — it *was* funny. I can see Joy's big smile and perfect teeth, hear her say, "He *what*?" shaking her head and laughing.

11
AN AD HOC MEMORIAL

When I first wrote this I could not have said on what day the memorial occurred — a day, or two, or three days after Joy died? In times of grief time expands, contracts, or simply collapses. I look back and see it was exactly five days later, but three days or five days make no difference when one is rising and falling through grief's choppy waters. Enough to say that it was too soon. Jane O'Keefe took over, and it could not have been easy. She'd lost Joy too, one of her best friends, but managed to be there for me. Seasoned by a string of her own losses, Jane knew how to help without me asking — something I could not do. I remember us discussing the idea of a memorial — *Is it too soon? Shouldn't I wait?* — but Jane encouraged me to do it sooner rather than later since we were not having a funeral. Of course if we'd had one it would have been just as fast; the Jews get you in the ground

74

quickly — too quickly I've always thought — though we make up for it by sitting shiva.

I picture the low wooden benches, the pieces of torn black fabric pinned to the mourners' shirts, my mother pale without makeup, my aunt Ruth, always the first to show up in bad times, cooking and cleaning, relatives crowded into the living room, telling stories: sitting shiva in my Long Island home for my uncle, my mother's brother, who had died on the operating table during what was then experimental open-heart surgery. He was thirty-six, leaving behind a young wife and two little boys.

It is a ritual I was to observe several times during my youth, a mix of terrifying (death brought into the home) yet comforting (my mother's large family, all of whom I liked, gathered together).

But I knew Joy would want none of this. She was a *modern girl* who disdained religion and its rituals.

Joy did not want a funeral, at least I don't think so. We never spoke of what she wanted because she refused to talk about dying, and I never imagined her death, only my own. With my family history of heart disease we were both convinced I would die first. We were, in fact, so convinced that we canceled

Joy's life insurance policy several years earlier.

Most of Joy's extended family had lived well into their nineties, though both her parents had been struck down by cancer in their seventies, something Joy feared but rationalized: they were unlucky, they were anomalies; though she was particularly fearful of the breast cancer that killed her mother and had regular checkups, every one incredibly fraught. I don't think she ever allowed herself to believe she would get the disease, but the fear was always there, lurking.

I have an indelible image of Joy's mother when she finally lost her protracted but brave battle against breast cancer, in the hospital, flanked by her daughters. "Girls," she said. "I'm sorry, but you have to let me go." I see both sisters' faces, but more so my sister-in-law's, then as now the brave big sister, and how she managed to say, "Okay, Mom," through her tears.

Joy mourned her mother quietly, as she did most things. There was very little discussion and she displayed little outward grief, though I knew she felt it.

Her father had died ten years earlier. At the time, Joy was four months pregnant. I remember we showed him an in utero photo of our daughter taken during amniocentesis, though I can't remember if he was well enough to see it. The birth of our daughter a few months later was the best distraction Joy could have had, if bittersweet — the fact that her father never got to see his grandchild. I'm not sure Joy ever dealt with her father's death; she rarely spoke of it.

When I lost my father, more than thirty years ago, I pretty much ignored it. He was a difficult, often distant man and I didn't think his death would have much impact on my life, and in the everyday way, that was true. I was already an adult, so he was not tied to the routine of my daily life in any way — it seemed the natural order, parent dying before child.

I had no idea I would miss my father because I so rarely talked to him in any meaningful way. But I was wrong. I still think about my father's death because I never truly looked at it, did not take in the enormity of it: that my one and only father had died.

I delivered the eulogy at his funeral, a task assigned to me by my mother.

"My father," I began, "has been preparing me for his death since I was fourteen, when he suffered his first heart attack. 'Jon,' he'd say, 'We all die. Do not make a big deal of it

77

when I do.' We had this conversation many, many times."

I paused and looked out over the roomful of mourners — aunts, uncles, cousins, friends, my sister, my mother.

"And so," I said, "I am *not* going to make a big deal of it. His body is out back, in a Hefty bag."

It was a risky joke but it cut through the tension and the entire congregation burst into laughter.

My father had very little sense of humor, though I think he would have laughed too. I know my mother did.

When the laughter died down, I continued on a more serious note. "My father was not an easy man. He was tough and uncompromising but he taught me many things, most importantly, never to quit and to face difficult situations head-on. One time, when his business was doing poorly, he spent a lot of money redecorating his showroom, and I asked him why. 'If you want to *be* successful, you have to *look* successful.' My father never gave up and never quit. He had much success and plenty of disappointments, all of which he shared with my mother. He spent his last day on earth as if he had planned it, playing a full round of golf before dancing with the woman he loved, then died in a matter of minutes. For him, it was a good death — though perhaps not so good for everyone else at the country club dance that night."

My mother was pleased with what I'd said and that was the point: I wanted to make her happy and I wanted to make my father proud, something I had always struggled with while he was alive.

Joy and I both had tough fathers. We sometimes wondered whether this had attracted us to one another, if there had been some innate flaw or need we sniffed out in the other. Joy often described her dad as a tyrant. As usual, I needed more words for mine: tough, cold, erratic, dark. Once, when I espoused the theory that women who had strong, supportive, loving fathers were usually more successful, Joy was hurt, though I hadn't been excluding her. Her father may have been tough, but he was also loving; I saw many examples of this over the years. "But not supportive," Joy said. "He didn't think I could do *anything*." I thought she was wrong, but how could I know; he wasn't my father and I hadn't been there when she was growing up, though I still believe he must have done something right because Joy was hardworking, steadfast, and ultimately very successful.

■ ■ ■ ■

I don't remember anything before Joy's memorial, not getting dressed, nor what I wore. I have no memory of showering or shaving though I'm sure I did.

I remember people showing up, soon a crowd of a hundred or more crammed from one end of our loft to the other, and me meeting and greeting and trying to smile.

A friend of Joy's, one I hardly knew, collapsed into my arms with such grief that I wanted to push her away — *This is too much! Stop, please!* — but I stood there with her sobbing against my chest, paralyzed, a confluence of emotions all pitched so high they canceled each other out until I felt nothing.

I remember talking to people without knowing what I was saying, the whole time a hazy filter over my senses, as if I were underwater, a sensation I would have quite a lot in the weeks to come.

I remember people giving speeches: one friend speaking of Joy's achievement in food history, another of how she always went to Joy to solve problems, yet another telling funny stories.

Then my mother steps forward. At ninety

she looks and acts twenty years younger, a former Roxy dancer, still a redhead (artificially), and petite. I never expected she would outlive my wife. She reads from a paper, her hand shaking — my mother is usually calm and collected. She says that in the forty years she has known Joy they have never had a single argument. She speaks of the unfairness of losing someone so much younger.

Everything is beautiful and heartfelt, as it should be, though it feels as if I am in a play.

Then it is my turn. I stand. I clear my throat. "I know Joy would say that I always speak at everything for everyone and so I had better say something about her."

I still wonder how I found the ability to speak.

"Joy and I have been married for more than forty years, children when we met, but we grew up together. Our marriage, like any, was not perfect but we made it work." I cite a friend, who said, "I always liked you, but when I met Joy I liked you more for having such a smart and interesting wife." Then I say, out loud, without meaning to, "Who will tell me what I'm doing wrong?" and people laugh, while I swallow hard fighting tears, because I had meant it quite seriously.

81

When I finish, it is as if everything has drained out of me, blood, breath. I feel shaky and quickly sit down.

After that, people came and went for a long time, but I can't remember any of those conversations.

Dorie recalls being cornered by one of my friends who showed her cell phone pictures of her daughter in a bikini and kept repeating how the daughter was so hot; she also remembers standing with her friends and laughing about something, thinking: *How can I be laughing?*

When everyone finally left, Dorie and I got into my bed and watched a movie.

Runaway Bride with Julia Roberts. We had started to watch something else, which was too serious, and turned it off after a few minutes.

I recently asked Dorie and she said we did not watch a movie that night, though there were several nights when we did. She thinks we watched a Julia Roberts movie, but not that one. She says it was *My Best Friend's Wedding,* or maybe it wasn't a Julia Roberts movie at all, but *The Devil Wears Prada.* Clearly, her memory concerning those days and events is as scrambled as mine.

■ ■ ■ ■

That night I take a sleeping pill, though only sleep in small fitful snatches. Each time I awake it takes a moment to know what is real and what is not, to understand that Joy has died.

Later in the night I think about the anniversary party we had in July, something I had not wanted but Joy insisted upon. *We have to celebrate the good things.* It was just our close friends, and it was in fact a very nice night. I see Joy in her dark crimson blouse, dangling Victorian earrings, and the reddish-brown lipstick she'd taken to wearing in the last few years. I made a toast about our many years together, how good they'd been and how lucky we were, and I recall being conscious of not making a joke because I knew Joy would not be happy if I did, that it was important I express the sentiment without my usual irony, and later she thanked me.

How long ago was this?

I am suddenly on my cell phone checking the calendar, counting the days and realizing that the anniversary party had been exactly thirty-nine days before Joy died. Now I am trying to remember what happened during that time. Was there anything important, significant, particularly sweet and tender between us or had we been fighting, and what, if anything, can I possibly do with this information except think of all the things I should have and could have done better, if only I had known. I squeeze my eyes shut against the thought, which only jump-starts the movie — paramedics, ambulance, hospital, Joy's face in death.

If only I had gone into the living room ten minutes earlier, my latest mantra, which has replaced *Everything will be okay,* because clearly everything was not.

I flick on the lights, slide my laptop onto my chest, and find something, anything, to watch, to distract myself — the beginning of a very bad habit — though the memorial comes back to me in a rush of overlapping images. All of it too fast, too soon for goodbyes and tributes, and surely too soon for me, in a fog that kept me apart, still the invisible man watching from a distance.

12
UNANSWERED QUESTIONS

A million times a day I thought: I have to ask Joy this, have to tell her that, but I could not ask the questions nor invent her answers. Though I knew my wife better than anyone — and I think she knew me — there are things we never know.

A lot of people talk to their dead spouse or parents and feel as if they get answers. I did not. The door of communication had slammed shut. The person with whom I'd lived for more than forty years was gone. I'd lost my sounding board, my reality check, my echo.

If that sounds egocentric, I think I was the same for Joy. There is, in the best coupling, the telling and retelling — the story of your day, the banalities that drift in and out of your mind that only take shape or have meaning when told and considered by the other, your partner.

I missed Joy's counsel in innumerable

ways. She was my in-house editor and art critic, who knew instinctively if it was encouragement I was after ("It's great, keep going") or real criticism ("There's something wrong with . . .").

Joy nursed my bruised ego when I needed it, but also told me when I'd overreacted or was being unreasonable, an invaluable Geiger counter that saved me from saying the wrong thing or from curling up with my hurt feelings, and I provided that for her too, though Joy was more sensitive when it came to my criticism. I edited her work but it was often like teaching your wife how to drive. She could take criticism from almost everyone, but not from me. I learned to read what she wrote, make suggestions and corrections, hand it back to her with a smile, then take cover! Joy may not have liked my criticism, but she continued to ask for it and respect it.

For most of Joy's adult life she'd been a business researcher with a specialty in the food world, a job she excelled at, but when Dorie went to college, so did she. Determined to change her life, she got a master's in food studies, then dove into the field, publishing articles and soon embarking on a book of epic proportions, *Food City: Four Centuries of Food-Making in New York.*

Once Joy established herself in the food history world she was a different person, stronger and more self-assured, with a new group of colleagues and a circle of food scholar friends.

Joy's reinvention was impressive, and totally her own. Though I went to her readings and events, I did not invade her world. I was not one of those husbands who bragged about his wife's achievements, though I was proud of her.

The great thing about living with another artist is that you do not have to explain yourself or the fact that you want/need time alone to pursue your work. It is a given. For many years Joy gave me that time and when she needed it I understood and was happy to step back and let her have it — and it was not about sacrifice. No matter what, Joy and I were never competitive about our work and always happy for each other's successes, not an easy thing to find in this world.

For the past decade, when we both worked at home, in our individual, soundproof offices, we came up with rules — no one could go into the other's office without permission, no lunch together — and we pretty much stuck with the no-lunch rule because it was easy: Joy ate lunch and I did not. But we interrupted each other all the time. Or rather, *I* interrupted Joy. I mean, I had questions! *What do you think of this — of that? Would you take a look at this e-mail before I send it? Do you think this drawing is any good?* I found a dozen reasons to interrupt Joy's work throughout the day and she did not complain though she rarely interrupted mine. Despite what some might call too much togetherness, there was a security in knowing that Joy was on the other side of the wall.

In the past, when we were apart, and there were plenty of times, we would call every day, and many of those calls were our best conversations. But now, there were no calls, no reporting, no roundup of daily events.

When I think about it, I'd say that what I came to miss most were the ordinary moments of our daily life, the in-between stuff when you don't know anything is happening, the infinite forgettable moments.

So how does one get past such a loss, the echoing silence — no planning, no resolutions, no arguments, no promises, no talking about dreams for the future? How is one supposed to accept that what has happened is true and irrevocable? That's the stunning part, that it's irrevocable. That the person you have lost is not coming back. *Ever.*

I'm not sure there is an answer of what to do about that. Some people, I know, turn to religion. Others, to drink. To get through the nights I took pills, which partially staved off insomnia and nightmares but left me jittery and hung over.

Perhaps, had I not been taking pills I might have been able to decipher the nagging question that would slip into my mind from time to time, the idea that I had missed something. But every time I got close the image would break up and disintegrate, though a vexing afterimage lingered, waiting to be decoded.

13
KEEPING A NOTEBOOK

It is the middle of the night and I am in my studio. In the past I have always loved being here at night, the quiet, the sense that the world has gone away and I can write or make art in solitude, but not tonight when I am sleep-deprived and edgy.

The first time we saw this loft it was early spring, one of those cool crisp days when you no longer need your winter coat and you feel hopeful, the nondescript Manhattan street transformed into a miraculous urban garden. A mirage, of course; the Flower District's impromptu garden disappeared by dusk, leaving the street naked and ugly, but we didn't know that yet. All we saw was greenery and color — in the middle of New York City — hundreds of gardenia plants, so beautiful and aromatic their fragrance wafted up to the fifth floor, the seller smart enough to have all of the windows open. "This is the place," Joy said while I took in the raw concrete floors, bare bulbs strung on wire, pitted brick walls with small patches of fur as if an animal had been chased through the place and had pieces of its pelt torn from its hide (it turned out the place had been a fur vault for forty years). But Joy was insistent. "We can do anything we want with it, make it our own," and she was right.

My studio still displays some of the loft's bare bones, the concrete floor, one brick wall enlivened only by artwork.

I begin sorting through my collection of unused notebooks and sketch pads, ones with leather covers, others with handmade paper, most given to me as gifts over the years and set aside, all of them too precious and intimidating, as if every word I'd write or sketch I'd make would have to be important. I choose the old-style composition notebook because it is ordinary and familiar, though I've no idea what I want to write in it.

My mind remains a shortwave radio, one that is picking up recent half thoughts and mixing them with images from the past: Joy and I taking our baby daughter home from the hospital in a hired limo though we had no money; an art gallery opening in Chelsea, Joy tossing me a smile across the jam-packed room, me knowing she is uncomfortable in a crowd but keeping that smile on her face because it is my show and we both must perform.

Joy's smile fades.

I open the notebook and write:

Get the names of the paramedics, so I can thank them.

(Something I never do, though I should have; they worked heroically, if in vain.)

Under that:

Track down the emergency room doctor.

(Which I have been trying to do, unsuccessfully.)

I turn a page and write about my friend Judd, how his visit comforted me, how he is always a calming influence, then about Jane O'Keefe, how she has *come to my rescue.*

I see Jane and Joy on the porch of Jane's country home and they are laughing. I see Dorie, six weeks old, asleep on Jane's chest, her first babysitter. Then Dorie in my kitchen the morning after Joy died, eyes sad and swollen.

I write and underline:

Worried about Dorie.

I put the pencil down and stare into the dark.

There is too much to say.

When I pick up the notebook again it will

be several days between writing that line about Dorie and my next entry, going to dinner with a friend. It is an inauspicious entry. *I said this. My friend said that. I was disconnected, not quite there, feeling sad.*

Prosaic scribble.

There are notes about trying to get the autopsy results and my increasing frustration. More notes about Dorie, worrying and wondering not only if she is okay but if she is mad at me, though I do not draw any conclusions.

I wrote in an automatic, almost hypnotic state.

It was quite a while before I became aware of what I was doing and when I did I had mixed feelings about writing about my wife's death, as if I didn't have the right, but the writing was not necessarily about her. It was about me: what I felt or didn't feel or couldn't feel.

"Men do not write books about grief" was something I heard a lot and even told myself.

But why not?

At one point, my daughter called me the "most unsentimental man ever," and that's true, on the outside, something I think is true for many men, who I believe are culturally conditioned to be stoic and unemotional but also conditioned to take care of their wives and partners and families, which may or may not be an outdated notion depending on your age or upbringing. How to balance these two conflicting objectives is, I think, one of the primary issues for men dealing with grief, or at least it was for me.

There are plenty of things men and women share, the basic fundamentals of human grief for one, but in keeping the notebook, I came to see that the expectations for grieving men as opposed to grieving women, the cultural lens through which they are viewed and treated, are very different. I never consciously looked at things through a man's point of view, but it's obviously who I am and the way I see things.

Sometimes what I wrote seems absurd, even funny, and of course sad. The thing is that death and grief are not so different from life, which is often absurd, funny, and sad. But loss heightens everything so that you actually *see* the absurd, funny, and sad moments; you watch them, often at a distance, yet everything is underscored or in high relief, as if someone is writing them on a blackboard or carving them into the side of a mountain.

As I reread the notebook entries I often see (in retrospect), how my responses to certain incidents were wrong; that is, how they were not at all helpful to me, or those around me.

I am not a fan of how-to manuals, and my notebook was never that. I claim no expertise in these matters, but this experience makes each of us an unwilling professional, an excavator in the dark mine of death, and perhaps my steps and missteps will provide some knowledge if not exactly answers for others.

14
STARTING TO DRAW

I started drawing around the same time I started writing in my notebook.

Unable to sleep, I am once again in my studio. For a while I sit at my L-shaped plywood desk, and do nothing. The studio feels foreign, as though I have no idea what I ever did in here.

I note that the photograph I have had of Joy and Dorie on my desk for years is missing and for a moment I forget that I was the one to remove it. I hate the fact that it's gone but can't bring myself to put it back, to look at it.

A friend who lost her husband told me that she put a large blowup photograph of him in the living room so that she could see and feel his presence. I did the opposite. Only days after Joy died I hid all of the photographs. I couldn't look at them without feeling unbearable grief, guilt, and a tumult of unsorted emotions.

I get up. I sit down. I get up again. I spend a long time lining up dozens of pencils on my drawing table, in order, from hard to soft, 2B through 8B. I put a new refill into one of the plastic eraser pens I like to use. It feels good to organize things when everything in my life feels out of control.

On impulse, I go into Joy's office, the first time since her death. I stand in the dim light and feel totally disconnected, weightless. I do not feel sad or bad or emotionally overwhelmed. I feel nothing until I realize I am holding my breath and my lungs are aching and I begin to shake. I want to bolt but I'm frozen, taking in the papers and books on Joy's desk, her pens and pads, her open laptop. I tap the keyboard and the screen lights up to a page of text, the cursor throbbing midsentence. I jerk back, once again wanting to flee but I am riveted, reading the typed words, then the xeroxed page of research beside the computer, a few sentences highlighted in yellow, everything exactly as Joy left it, as if she is on a short break and will be back any moment.

I spy the mock-up cover for her book, the title in bold, **Food City**, and the phrase that came to me in the hospital, *life's work,* flickers in my brain, and then I am feeling things: regret, sadness, a deep hollow aching inside me. I make a vow that no matter what, the unedited four-hundred-thousand-word manuscript Joy has left behind will be published.

Among the many papers on her desk is a grainy black-and-white picture Joy has printed out from her computer. I stare at it a moment but it is too much for me to take in, not like this. I pluck it off the desk and head back to my studio where I prop it up on my drawing table, study it for a moment, then begin to approximate it in pencil on paper. I go back and forth between the printout and my drawing, conscious of what I'm doing until I lose track of time. Soon, I have enough "information" in my drawing so that I no longer need to look at the source. I keep drawing, filling in details, unaware of the time. Then I sit back.

I stare at the drawing I made from the printout — it is from an author photo Joy had taken not long before her death.

Surprisingly, it has not been difficult to study the facsimile and make a drawing from it. I'd look at the source material for a few seconds at a time, dissect it, then re-assemble and re-create the image on the page. Without thinking, I knew Joy would want me to soften her chin and make sure her eyes did not look puffy, and I did those

things while the other half of my brain concentrated on the mark, the line, the tone, as I would in any other drawing.

I am able to draw my wife because drawing is abstract, because you can't really draw something until you stop identifying it. You can't think: this is an eye, or a nose, or lips, or you will not be able to draw them; an eye, a nose, lips are all the same, simply marks on a page.

Drawing has made it possible for me to stay close to Joy when she is no longer here. It is a way to create a picture of her without feeling weird or maudlin. I am not sitting in a dark room crying over a photo of my dead wife; I am at my drawing table, working.

Grief is chaotic; art is order. Ironic, as most people think art is all about *feeling* and *emotion,* when in fact the artist needs to be ordered and conscious to create art that will, in turn, stir feelings and emotion in others.

Artists are perpetually engaged in the act of fixing their broken worlds and this has been the case with me for most of my life, and now more so than ever.

I was trained as a visual artist and it is the way I see the world — in pictures. When I want to write something I usually picture it first, then find the words to describe it.

When I am drawing, time is suspended and it calms me, forces me to stop whatever I am doing — fidgeting, worrying — to get my hand and eye coordinated.

Drawing not only makes me pause, catch my breath, and look, it allows me to make something out of my sadness.

My graduate school painting teacher, the wonderful artist George McNeil, a founding member of the American Abstract Artists way back in 1936, a man I adored and admired, always told us, his students, to take

100

our anger and sorrow, all of our angst, and "put it into your work." Good advice. It is what I am trying to do now: take my sorrow and grief and give it form.

Of course there were many instances, actual events where drawing was of no use, where I could not suddenly whip out a pencil, stand back, observe, and document the moment in a sketch. Sometimes the stunning reality of what had happened did just that: it stunned me.

15
GUILT

My wife had died and I could not save her.

There it is, the truth, and no way around it.

For months I was infused with guilt.

In dreams, I'd see my wife beckoning to me and do nothing.

I continually asked myself why did I not come into the living room earlier? Why did I not insist we go to the hospital the moment her cheeks flushed and her leg started twitching?

Because she had called the doctor's office and they said it was nothing to worry about. I think about that now and shudder because they made a tragic mistake — and this was not the only one.

Another new mantra: *I should have done something.*

Is it that men are brought up with the idea that they can fix everything? (An absurd notion, but one I had at least partially subscribed to until proven wrong.)

Or is it survivor guilt? *Why her and not me?*

Perhaps a little of both.

Guilt prevented me from enjoying a good meal or good times with friends. It took me months to go to a movie because movies were one of Joy's favorite things. When I finally went, I left midway through; I simply could not sit there.

My guilt was unbearable. I bowed down to it and let it take charge.

It didn't matter that my internist told me there was nothing I could have done. It didn't matter that another doctor friend said exactly the same thing.

I thought: *But they don't know I was in the next room — that if I had gone in ten minutes earlier I might have saved her.*

My brother-in-law said he was sorry he hadn't been there because he would have done something. He didn't mean it in a bad way, I know that; it was his frustration talking. And though I said nothing, certainly not to my sister-in-law, who was going through her own grief and hell, I wanted to rip his heart out. How dare he suggest that if *he'd* been there *he* could have saved Joy when I could not?

The worst part? He was expressing exactly

what I'd been feeling — that somehow I *should* have been able to save her.

The few friends I told about my guilty feelings tried to assuage me or suggested therapy, but I wasn't ready to talk about it. Plus, a part of me did not want someone to tell me that I had not done anything wrong, to exonerate me.

Here it is, what I figured out: a part of me needed to suffer.

Suffering was painful and tangible but something I could curl up with, and I did. I replayed the day constantly: I'd picture my wife on the other end of the loft, a hundred feet away, cell phone in hand, unable to speak, trying to reach me.

I tortured myself with this scenario for which there was no resolution, only acceptance: this is what happened, this is what you did and did not do, there is no turning back the clock.

This narrative of guilt stayed with me for a long time, tackling me at unexpected times during the day, and always at night.

There were times I became my own drill sergeant. *Shape up! Dump the guilt! Everyone loses someone. Everyone dies. Get on with your life!* But the pep talk only made me feel worse.

I'd taught my daughter my rule regarding

disappointment, one I had developed over the years that made it possible to survive as an artist: allow yourself exactly one hour to feel bad about a rejection or disappointment. That is, for one hour you can really wallow in it — cry, scream, get under the bed and suck your thumb, throw things, stomp around and curse. But that's it. Then you have to let it go.

I tried to apply this regimen to my grief, but the scale of this loss not only trumps disappointment and rejection, it makes you realize how trivial and frivolous they are.

If I were a therapist, I would say understand there was nothing you could have done and accept the fact that you will feel guilty and that it will ease in time. I would say that feeling guilty is inevitable but unnecessary: there is no reason for you to suffer from guilt — you are already suffering enough. I would say, stop punishing yourself with the *What if*s and *If only*s. And I think that's all very solid advice. But if I can't convince myself, how can I possibly convince others?

It is certainly possible that a therapist would be a better route for some, and possibly for me. Therapy has helped me in the past. But I did not want, nor could I possibly imagine, a "talking cure."

So what then?

It took a while to see that I was processing it here, on the page, by writing it all down and for now, that is my therapy. My drawing too, which, one could say, is my occupational therapy — something that has worked for me for most of my life.

As a kid, I was always drawing. It was a place for me to escape and get lost. Something I excelled at, and there weren't many areas where I did. I was a mediocre student, a classic "underachiever," a dreamer who could not concentrate on history or math, though I made elaborate drawings of experiments in my biology and chemistry notebooks.

Drawing got me through a lot. I was a terrible athlete, which instantly set me apart from the other boys, and from my father, who was a great athlete. I remember him coming to school (a rarity) to speak to my junior high gym teacher.

"Can't you *do* something with him?" my father asked the teacher, an amiable man, one of the few gym teachers who was nice to me (or perhaps took pity on me).

"Your son has many fine qualities but athletics is not one of them," he said. "I suggest you take pride in the things he does well."

Standing beside my father I was filled with conflicting feelings of pride and shame. I didn't say anything to my father, then or later, nor did he.

I was brought up to hide my feelings. My mother, a wonderfully upbeat person, simply does not allow sad things to affect her and it's something she has tried (and mostly failed) to pass on to her children. The idea of wailing or keening is so far from her repertoire of good cheer that I'm sure she finds it an embarrassment or simply alien. That is *not* to say that she is unfeeling or unsympathetic. She is caring and very sympathetic. She simply doesn't allow sadness in. I have some of her resilience but it's coupled with a good deal of my father's negativity. I used to say it was impossible to locate your feelings in a household where one parent was all white, the other all black.

And it became almost impossible for me now. I could not locate nor separate my feelings of grief from guilt, nor guilt from loss, nor sadness from depression — all of those feelings roiling around, though guilt often managed to find its way to the surface and ride the waves.

The flip side of guilt is self-pity.

It's the danger inherent in all grieving, feeling sorry for yourself. On occasion, I can separate my sorrow from self-pity, but the two play a good game of catch and at worst go hand in hand. It's hard, once you've allowed yourself to go down the self-pity road, to do an about-face because wallowing in self-pity is such sweet agony. And yet, the idea of anyone feeling sorry for me is truly abhorrent. Remember, I am, and was, very busy keeping up all appearances of manly reserve.

Guilt was hard to avoid and get over, and it still, on occasion, crawls inside my head and whispers all sorts of bad stuff. The only thing I can do is not listen.

And yet, one needs to listen, to pay attention, because there are important things to be heard, and to be done. However painful, it's better to be at least partially conscious, to feel the pain rather than pretend it's not happening. Better to have painful memories than to have no memories at all.

16
IN THE CLASSROOM

Joy had died on August 16. My college teaching was set to resume two weeks later. No one expected me to do it. For a while I didn't think I would, or could. But I did.

It was somewhat surreal to be in a classroom with students who had no idea my life had changed completely, but not at all strange to be talking about writing or how to illustrate stories, things I have been talking about for years.

For the hours that I taught, when I was thinking about my students and not myself, I felt truly okay, the one time I was not caught up in my own grief, and it was the best thing I did. I was not only fulfilling my commitment (I was brought up to believe that you fulfilled your obligations no matter what), but it gave me a reason to wake up in the morning and was thoroughly distracting while I was doing it.

I had my classes at Pratt and my crime-writing workshops at the Center for Fiction. My Pratt undergrads had no idea what had happened, though I think I was more philosophical than usual, and perhaps they wondered why. Some of my students at the Center knew that my wife had died, as they had become friends, and offered condolences, which I accepted, then quickly changed the subject. I could not risk cracking my well-crafted reserve in public.

Teaching was the primary stage on which I practiced and became quite adept at impersonating my former self. When I was doing a good job of it, I almost forgot I was acting.

More than ever I found myself relying on humor — I couldn't stand playing the wounded husband or sufferer (even though a part of me wanted sympathy, receiving it was next to impossible). You don't change your personality just because your spouse or partner dies. If you were funny (and I think I was — sometimes) you're still funny, at least outwardly; I didn't develop my ironic sense of humor for nothing: it got me through a problematic childhood and adolescence and it helped me now, though sometimes I saw it had the opposite effect of what I'd intended — to cut through sadness or an uncomfortable moment. Instead, it made some people think I was callous. A woman I teach with said, "I don't know how you're teaching, how you're even here. If *my* husband had died I'd be in bed, unable to *move,*" and she didn't say it out of admiration but with a look of disapproval, as if I were not suffering enough. I wanted to say, *You have no idea what I'm feeling, the depths of my sadness, nor do you have any idea if you will be in bed or ice-skating when your husband dies.* I managed a strained smile and walked away.

The rewards of teaching were never more apparent. The give-and-take, imparting whatever knowledge I've acquired over the years, seeing my students improve and succeed.

I've always said that teaching keeps you honest by forcing you to think and question things you have long taken for granted. And now it kept me going, interacting with students, with life, participating.

During this time the only writing I did was connected to my teaching. At any other point in my life if I'd felt teaching had usurped my own writing time I'd have been resentful. But not now.

There was other work, commissioned paintings, which I've been doing for years and I like doing them, though they were more difficult because it is work done mostly in isolation, when I was at my most vulnerable. But I did it; in fact, I took on more commissions than I normally would because I needed to keep busy.

The thing about work is that something is expected of you and you have to do it. Before Joy died, the days I had nothing to do but my *own* work were blissful. Now, I needed *assignments* — teaching, painting commissions, short stories for anthologies. Without something specific I found it nearly impossible to work. I could not pursue art or writing for the sake of itself, which for me had always been the sign of a true artist or writer, that you did your work no matter what. Now I needed projects, goals.

The one thing I did for myself was to begin working on an illustrated children's book, something I had always wanted to do. It started with a couple of drawings and a simple plot and grew, page after page, drawings stacking up, then tacked to my studio walls until they filled three. The book became a good place for me to escape, a world of adventure geared toward children, and one I liked going into.

The enduring transformative power of art continued to nourish and amaze me.

One day, going through a box of articles

and reviews, I found the research I'd done for an article on art and aging I'd written years ago for *ARTNews*. I listened to the taped interviews I'd made with the artists, all in their eighties and nineties, and it comforted me to hear them talk about adapting to old age and infirmities, to change and loss. The artist Hedda Sterne (the only woman in the famous 1951 *Life* magazine photograph of the "Irascibles," which included such luminaries as Jackson Pollock and Willem de Kooning) saying how painting had sustained her for more than seventy years; the artist Milton Resnick telling me that when his aging aching knees made it impossible for him to paint standing up he sat, hired models, and it changed the abstract paintings he'd been making for decades into totally new paintings that contained a human figure.

In the same box I found a postcard sent to me by a museum curator when I'd lost ten years of paintings in a gallery fire. The fire hadn't quite registered at first (I am beginning to see that's the way loss works), but after a week or two it hit me — a decade of artwork up in smoke, and I was stunned by the idea that my paintings were gone forever.

I look at the postcard now, a picture of

Gustave Courbet's *The Stone Breakers,* a painting destroyed during World War II, turn it over, and read what the curator has written on the back: *This painting is gone but not forgotten.*

It was the most thoughtful and meaningful thing anyone could have said to me at the time and I cherished it.

A couple of months after the gallery fire I replicated Courbet's *The Stone Breakers* in pencil on paper, but reduced in size to a foot square. In front of the painting I drew a portrait of the artist, Courbet, copied from a nineteenth-century photograph. At the time, I considered it an homage to the artist. Now I realize it was my way of coping with the loss of *my* paintings, not Courbet's, proving to myself that a lost painting could exist again. Clearly, drawing as coping has been with me for a long time. When I had my next exhibition I hung the small drawing alone on a large wall, but it was not for sale. It still hangs in my living room.

That gallery fire changed my life.

Frustrated with painting, I started writing and it felt good to be teaching myself something new, to express myself in some other way, an example of what I have been espousing: that one can always find alternative ways to be creative. After the fire, writing calmed me when I could not draw or paint, and it made me see that it was possible to start over.

I am no stranger to reinvention; it is, in fact, something I believe in. It was not easy to lose a decade of artwork and I don't recommend a fire, but the loss forced me to try something new, to make yet another leap of faith with my writing. And it made me brave. I think about what Joy said to me at the time: *If you put your mind to it you can do anything.* Not true, but it's clear why I loved her.

The idea of reinvention hovers beneath loss and grief: *I am alone and will have to figure out what that means, figure out who I am now, and what comes next.*

This is not, or was not, a conscious thought until I wrote it down in my notebook several months after Joy had died, but I think it's true. To survive the loss I will have to change. The old me, the coupled me, no longer exists, and the single me needs to go forward. It's what I have been struggling to do, though it is an unconscious process, like the body healing a cut or a bruise — it just starts to do it, with or without your cooperation.

115

17
TWO KIDS PLAYING GROWN-UP

It is two in the morning and I am unable to sleep. I have been surfing Netflix for over an hour, in bed, unable to watch anything for more than five minutes, the laptop on my chest getting hot, and I worry it has to be unhealthy. I slide a pillow under the computer, and surf some more.

After a while, I give up and move to the living room where I attempt to reread favorite passages of a Billy Wilder biography, the great film director recounting his impossible times trying to direct Marilyn Monroe, fifty-six takes to say "It's me, Sugar."

In the past, reading calmed me when I could not sleep, now I can hardly read at all, my eyes and mind unable to concentrate on anything for more than a few minutes before the words blur and my mind wanders.

I look for another book and spy the box that contains our wedding photos, which has been in the bookcase for decades. For a moment, I consider looking at them, then immediately change my mind: no way I can face all those photographic memories.

But I know what I can do.

I unearth our framed "official" wedding photo, which I have hidden in a drawer, and take it into the studio where I study it in fragments only, then reinterpret those fragments on the page in pencil marks. But no matter how abstract I try to keep the image it brings back my wedding day, sharp and clear.

Joy and I were so young when we married we had no idea what we were doing or what being married meant. Perhaps that's why it worked — because it was a seat-of-your-pants sort of arrangement.

We hadn't wanted a big wedding, had planned something small in my parents' backyard because Joy's parents had sold their New Jersey home and moved to Florida. Then, my parents' house burned down, dramatic and inconvenient, so we got married in a Long Island wedding factory by a rabbi who didn't know us, who stumbled over our names and pronounced *love* as *lurve,* so that we couldn't look at each other for fear of laughing; this, as we took our vows.

After the wedding, in our continuing ad hoc way, we just got in the car and drove. We'd made no plans, surely none for a honeymoon, the apartment we had rented, in Brooklyn, had no bed, the mattress being delivered on Monday, and it was Saturday.

We couldn't believe we were actually married. Joy said she was glad to have something to call me other than "my boyfriend" and we tried out a variety of sentences using "my husband" and "my wife," all of which seemed hilarious and absurd.

Stuck in traffic on the Long Island Expressway, we recognized that we had gotten into the car with no destination in mind. Relieved to be away from the reception, we'd changed out of our wedding clothes — my store-bought Edwardian suit with its narrow waist and bell-bottom pants, Joy's white lace mini that she had designed and my father's dress company made (despite my father's disapproval of a *mini* wedding gown) — and bolted.

We decide to keep driving.

Joy tells me how her oldest friend, Judy, asked her to hold her purse while she danced. "Like I wasn't even the bride," she says and laughs.

118

I tell Joy that my gambler uncle, my father's ne'er-do-well older brother (who, years later, was gunned down in a transient hotel), told me that he had several bets going at the wedding as to how soon we'd split up. He'd bet a hundred dollars we'd last less than a year. Joy was incredulous. I said, "Welcome to the family." (On our first anniversary I sent my uncle a check for a hundred dollars, as a joke — which he cashed!)

In the city, we looked for a hotel and realized, after trying four, all full, that somehow we had missed the fact that it was the Fourth of July.

But the big Hilton Hotel, on Sixth Avenue in the Fifties, had a room.

When the valet took our car, a modest white Rambler that my father had bought us as a wedding gift, a dozen empty coffee cans I collected to use for paintbrushes spilled out and banged around in the hotel's circular driveway. People stopped and stared. Joy and I could not stop laughing.

That night, in our big corporate-looking hotel room (which we loved because it was so unlike our life), we ordered room service. Joy had filet of sole with green grapes. I had a burger. We drank champagne. After that, we went to a movie, *Rosemary's Baby,* the perfect newlywed film. When we got back to the hotel we debated having sex because we were tired (it wasn't a huge deal, as we'd been having sex for almost two years), but we did, because it seemed like *not* having sex on your wedding night was bad luck.

On Monday we went to Con Edison and had the gas and electric turned on in our Brooklyn apartment.

All of this has been going through my mind as I sketched.

The photographer who took this picture, a friend of ours, took many good photos (all black-and-white — our "arty" choice) before he got drunk and took a lot of the floor, several of my sister's feet and none of her face, and many blurry shots of people dancing. Earlier in the evening he had the idea to shoot us looking formal and old-fashioned and we posed appropriately: two kids playing grown-up.

I distinctly remember posing for this picture, how I tucked Joy's hair behind her ear before the picture was shot and noticed the daisies she'd had entwined in her hair earlier were wilting. I remember she touched up her "nude" lipstick, and that my fitted jacket felt tight, even though I was skinny, and that I smoked a lot of cigarettes and Joy made me promise that I'd quit (which I

did — five years later).

I look at the drawing, two young people starting a life together, and I think: Now I am beginning one alone.

18
ORPHANS

Today the funeral home looks even more like a stage set, harsh sun creeping around the edges of the heavy drapes illuminating a tableau not meant to be seen in daylight. I stare at dust motes doing a slow dance in the streaks of light.

The too-cheery girl is not in. Instead, a dour-looking man, appropriately funereal, has me sign papers.

It is only a few days after the memorial. This time, Dorie is with me.

The man hands me a sealed cardboard box containing ashes — ashes that used to be my wife; that used to be Dorie's mother.

I ask him whether or not he knows if the autopsy was performed. He says he has no idea and gives the box a sideways glance, his features slightly screwed up. I get it: it's a little late for me to be asking.

Dorie and I leave quickly. We take a cab up Sixth Avenue, a short distance, though it feels interminable. We do not speak, the two of us cocooned inside our own minds, thoughts spinning and weaving though I am not ready to share them, and apparently neither is Dorie.

When we get home we are all business, discussing what we should do with the ashes. We consider burying them at our upstate home but decide against it, as I am already thinking I may sell it.

For now it seems appropriate, at least temporarily, to put Joy's ashes in her office, on her desk, among her books and papers.

I say temporarily because Dorie and I will soon arrive at a plan for them. It may be illegal but we are thinking that one day soon we will head over to the Hudson River, to a place where we walked several times in the weeks after Joy died, a place Joy and I liked to walk too, where you can see a wide swath of the river including the Statue of Liberty, and there, after dark, bequeath Joy's ashes to water.

I see Joy and me on those many walks, something we liked to do mostly in spring or fall, when the city was awakening from the winter or shutting down after summer, strolling from our loft to the waterfront, often hand in hand (after forty years of marriage we still liked to walk holding hands), talking about nothing special, those forgettable conversations and moments I miss.

It was, of course, very different when Dorie and I took this same walk in the aftermath of Joy's death.

I watch us from above, two orphans heading west along Twenty-Eighth Street, past warehouses and newly built condos, father and daughter walking with purpose when we both feel some portion of purpose has been taken from us. It is one of those late-summer afternoons when the sky is hazy and the city feels both tranquil and exhausted and we are straining to talk about little things that no longer matter.

We cross over the West Side Highway and there are people sunbathing on the narrow grassy slopes that lead to the river, several men in bikinis slathered in grease as if they are at the beach, not yards from a highway and skyscrapers. We can't help but make fun of them and it provides some release. We are still very much in shock but do not speak about our feelings of loss, only of our shared disbelief in its reality. We are walking together and there is comfort in that, having each other there, but we grieve privately. It is as if we are new people with new identities: the daughter without a mother, the husband without a wife.

I glance over at Dorie, taller than I, thin, wind whipping up her blond hair, the way she swipes it behind her ears, her face a composite — my eyes and Joy's full lips — and I think how Joy used to say that Dorie had chosen wisely, the best of each of us combined in a totally new and beautiful way.

Perhaps Dorie wants to talk about her mother's death, but in my ongoing quest for stoicism, I don't make room for that conversation, something that soon becomes a pattern. It wasn't just that I was not emotionally up to talking about it (I wasn't), or that I couldn't take hearing or seeing my daughter in pain (I couldn't), but I was so busy working overtime at keeping a mask on my face and a lid on my emotions I didn't dare lift the mask or open the lid — even if it meant putting distance between myself and my daughter, though I did not consider that in the moment and had no idea that it possibly would, or could.

But I think it did, a little, even as we grew closer.

In my defense, I will say that I was busy protecting Dorie from pain — and that was true, for both of us, I worried about her and she worried about me — but Dorie was in the throes of *two* major losses, her mother's death and a failed marriage, a lot of loss and pain for a young woman to carry.

I think back and realize that Dorie did not come to either me or Joy to discuss the problems of her marriage until she'd left it, and it makes me wonder if I have taught her too well to hide her feelings or if she simply inherited my ability to go silent and stoic in the face of unhappiness.

I had been trained well.

When I was growing up, my parents never told me if anything was wrong, not the severity of my father's first heart attack (he was not expected to live), not when his business failed and he was facing bankruptcy. I see my father in the hospital, oxygen mask on his face, a frightening image for a fourteen-year-old; and I see him at night, no matter what time I have come home or awakened, always in the den, wide-awake and worrying in the blue haze of late-night television. It produced in me a kind of nonspecific anxiety that despite what appeared to be good times, things were *not* good.

I created my own version of my mother's cheerful disposition in the face of trouble or even misfortune, the ability to make jokes while feeling terrible, an (almost) impenetrable facade of good cheer when in fact I am a worrier of epic proportions.

We are on the path along the Hudson when Dorie turns to me and says, "You can't die, okay?" Her eyes are watery but she forces a smile.

I say, "I'll do my best."

When Dorie was a teenager and I would say something she didn't like I'd kid her that it was good ammunition for future therapy. Now I'm thinking it's not so funny. Interesting too that both Dorie and I eschewed therapy after Joy died, neither of us feeling there was anything anyone could tell us that would help.

I don't mean any of this to sound as if we didn't lean on one another; we did, a lot, though I constantly worried about leaning on my daughter too much. (I mean, what sort of man does that?)

In the first weeks and months after Joy died, Dorie and I worried about each other in a way that was urgent and tangible. When she traveled (and she often did for work), I was insistent that she text me the minute her plane touched down, something Joy, the fearful flyer, always demanded. One day, Dorie tried to reach me, but I was out and had left my phone at home. By the time we made contact, five or six hours later, she was frantic, close to tears, and she made me promise I would always let her know where

I was. This particular kind of urgency eased after a while, but our collective worry remained potent.

On another day, not far from now, Dorie and I will take a walk along the High Line, the narrow strip of park built on the remains of an old elevated railroad line that overlooks the Hudson River, a place popular with tourists, but today it is not crowded. I am reminded that Joy was in the very early planning stages of a food-related piece with the well-known performance artist Ann Hamilton, to be installed on the High Line; they had met once and Joy had liked Ann very much, but the idea had either stalled or evaporated and now there was no chance of it happening, at least not with Joy's participation. I am about to bring this up when Dorie suggests a father/daughter road trip to the Southwest, a part of the country she has never seen, something, she says, we can do at Thanksgiving, as we are both dreading the holiday, Joy's favorite.

"Maybe we could write about it for a magazine," Dorie says.

We kick that idea around for most of our walk, a way to talk about Joy without really talking about her.

"We'll each keep diary entries," Dorie says.

"And I can do drawings to accompany the text."

Later, I contact the editor I'd worked with at *Travel + Leisure* and make my pitch: father and daughter take to the road to deal with their grief through travel, the parallel diary entries, my drawings to illustrate the piece.

The editor says no; she thinks it will be "too sad."

I thought she was wrong then and still do, but one rejection is all Dorie and I can handle at the moment, neither of us with the stamina to push the idea any further. Too bad, as I think it would have been a good thing for us to do, a way for us to deal with Joy's death in print, a lot easier than in discussion.

Later, when we took that Southwest trip, Dorie did keep a diary, though I've never seen it.

Dorie and I reach the river's edge. We lean against the railing, neither of us speaking. It is totally unlike the walks Joy and I took to this exact place, when we too leaned against the railing, enjoyed the scene, and had no need to talk. Now, as Dorie and I look down at the water, dark, deep, and opaque, it feels like a mirror of the conversation we are *not* having, at least not yet.

19
A PLACE FOR THE ASHES

Two nights later I am standing in Joy's office staring at the box of ashes. I feel an overwhelming need to find a better place for them, someplace safe, someplace appropriate. But what does that mean? How is any of this *appropriate*?

Joy's office is dark. I flip on the light and it's as if I have spotlit a crime scene — all of her books and papers frozen in time, an orange highlighter, cap off, drying out beside a large rectangular magnifying glass, one I'd had for looking at contact sheets (when I flirted with being a photographer after graduate school), and had given to Joy so she could read the tiny print in articles and old books.

I scoop the magnifying glass off her desk and hold it in my hand. It's old-fashioned and heavy, with a Bakelite handle and thick glass, a kind of talisman, a treasure trove of memory. I see myself buying it in the long-extinct photo shop in Herald Square and a series of photos I took — Joy done up like a model, false eyelashes and a feather boa wrapped around her neck, not at all the way she looked in real life, though she had fun dolling up and so did I taking the pictures. (Dorie, who has made a life in fashion, has a print from this day in her apartment: her mother as a glamour-puss.)

I look up and take in the framed photos Joy has lined up on a shelf above her desk, photographs I have seen hundreds of times and had not thought to hide: Dorie as a baby, Dorie at her college graduation, one of me and Joy from the late seventies, I recognize the living room of our two-story Hoboken loft, picture my street-level studio and remember our three cats, one an unruly stray who found her way to our front door and never left. A short comic movie plays in my mind: the stray cat swiping a leg of lamb off our kitchen table and dragging it down the long flight of stairs to the studio, chasing after her whooping and hollering as the lamb came to rest beside the cat box, coated with two inches of dust and dirt and sprinkled with kitty litter. I say, "Let's wash it off." Joy looks at me appalled. "Are you *kidding*?" I hadn't been but then we are both looking at the gross leg of lamb and Joy is shaking her head and then we are laughing.

I want to make a new drawing, one of Joy and me from that time.

Tucked into the edge of one of the framed photos is a tiny wallet-sized picture worn and torn in a few places from exactly this period of our lives. I take it back to my studio and tape it to a piece of cardboard to keep it from curling.

I squint at it and sketch rapidly, breaking things into simple shapes going from large to small, from general to specific, not stopping to evaluate what I have drawn. Then I slow down, get lost in the details, even draw in the tape, the tears, the shadows, something I have done in my "art" drawings for years, a way to suggest reality.

I look at my drawing and think we were a pretty cool-looking couple, and we really looked like this: Joy with her amazing thick, auburn hair, which changed often — long, short, pulled back, fluffed up — and me with the mustache that covered half my face. I like the way we gaze at each other in the drawing, Joy's assessing eyes and half smile. We were so young and in love in a way that was fresh and naive and like all young people never imagined we'd get old.

I wonder why I can look at my drawings and not photographs and it strikes me that

photos are static, whereas drawings are set in motion by the hand that draws them and so they take on a feeling of life, which is what I need to hold on to now.

At the time we lived in Hoboken. Joy hated being alone in that loft, the building isolated on a deserted backstreet, no other apartments, Pablo's Towing Station next door, and a low-income housing project a few blocks away.

During those years I was in an art performance group, the Mighty Oaks, led by Marcia Tucker, a Whitney Museum curator, who had become a good friend. I wanted Joy to join too, but she begged off with her usual disclaimer: *I am not a performer.*

I picture our little theater group changing clothes communally, seeing one another naked, surprised by Marcia's tattoos (around her nipples and more), long before anyone and everyone sported tattoos. After Marcia wrote the introduction to the 1976 book *Heavily Tattooed Men and Women,* which bestowed high-art praise on the tattoo artist Spider Webb, everyone in our performance group got tattooed, except me. Joy hated them. She didn't say I couldn't get one — "It's your body," she said — but I think it's good she stopped me; with my obsessive personality I'd have been tattooed from head to foot by now.

One night our weekly rehearsal in Marcia's SoHo loft went late, past two in the morning. I'd lost track of time and had neglected to call Joy, who finally called Marcia, in tears, imagining I had been in an accident and was lying dead somewhere. I was annoyed, embarrassed that my *wife* was calling to check up on me (which was, in fact, totally unlike Joy). I expected that Marcia, an independent, staunch feminist, might be annoyed too — and she was, at *me.* After that, Marcia made a point of reminding me to call if we ran late, and she and Joy soon became friends, bonding (good-naturedly) over my thoughtlessness. Marcia was dynamic and magnetic, and I realize now how Joy was often attracted to women whose personalities were unlike her own.

The Mighty Oaks performed a satiric piece, *The Best of Death, a Musical,* all in song. I sang "Teen Angel," the 1960 cornball teenage death song, a cappella in my highest tenor. (A Polish voice instructor worked with the group, and was always telling me to "sing from the top of your head, not through your nose!" She also accused me of hiding behind my mustache.) I managed to persuade Joy to sing backup for me, and she did, though she was very nervous about singing. She put on white lipstick and lots of black eyeliner and teased her hair and wore a miniskirt and knee-high boots, and later in the show she led a dance medley (she was a great dancer), the Hitchhike, the Pony, the Twist, and her specialty, the Mashed Potato, and she was a revelation, not the shy girl everyone thought she was; she even surprised me.

The image of Joy dancing fades as I come out of my reverie and stare at the box of ashes. It looks so inconsequential. I can't imagine it is all that remains of the girl in the beige jumper, the young woman I married, the mother of our daughter, the food historian, the author, the great dancer, my best friend.

I tug a few books out of Joy's crowded bookcase and push others aside. I slide the box of ashes in between a book on hardtack crackers in the Civil War and one about early sugar refining in New York. I think she will be happy between them.

I gaze at the box for another moment, then turn off the light. Just before closing the office door, I say, "Okay?" as if asking Joy if she likes the placement.

20
A Duo, Then a Threesome

There are many things to say about Joy that come easily to mind. She was solid and smart, an avid reader who worked hard to become a writer in midlife, a mother, and a very good one. She was earthy and sexy, without pretension. A woman who loved cardigan sweaters and expensive low-heeled shoes. A great dancer and a very bad singer. A loner but a loyal friend. A great listener but not the best talker. She hated to fight but rarely gave in. She loved planning trips and vacations more than going on them. She collected McCoy pottery and Victorian jewelry compulsively, and was passionate about movies. She wasn't funny but the best audience for anyone who was, and she never stopped thinking I was funny (an amazement). She loved her daughter, me, and her cat, Lily, in that order (though it's possible the cat came before me).

There were times my constant jabber

drove her crazy, though most of the time she claimed to enjoy it. Sometimes her reticence drove me nuts, but I usually found it soothing. We were often together for long periods of time (in a room, in the car) without speaking, but it was a good silence, not some angry brooding one. There was, between us, a psychic extension, an emotional cord that needed no explanation, like breathing, inhale, exhale, a back-and-forth without words, a comforting connection.

A memory comes to me, years ago, Joy and me driving through the Arizona desert, and how I was constantly remarking on the ever-changing landscape. At some point (we'd been in the car for days) I asked Joy if I was making her crazy with my nonstop travelogue.

"No," she said, "it's like the radio."

"In a good way, or bad?"

"Well, I'm only listening to half of it," she said. "Is that okay?"

It was.

Forever after, when I would talk on and on, Joy would ask, "Is this radio talk, or something I should listen to?"

Like all couples and good friends we had our shorthand too, half sentences, key words or phrases that meant nothing to anyone else that we immediately *got*, that could send one or the other of us into spasms of laughter.

As the years passed we managed to maintain our separate identities, though linked in a way that was physical, emotional, and practical. We made every important decision together, and thousands of trivial ones.

Joy kept me real. That is, she kept me honest about who I was because she saw me and knew me. For too much of my life I have felt as if I've worn disguises: the son who kept everyone in the family laughing when things were not funny, the cool artist, the outgoing guy who just wanted to be alone. Joy saw all of this about me, and more. She often admired my ability to wear so many disguises, but liked me best without them. That's not to say she liked or loved everything about me. I mean, who feels that way about *anyone*?

When you're in a relationship for as long as we were, you're kept on track by constant interaction, even simple physical proximity. Your partner keeps you sane (at least mine did) by questioning your actions and motives, and by forcing you to interact and compromise. It's a humanizing process, and for men the process is even more specific. I always say (only half-joking) that women civilize men, and I believe there's truth in that. I would sometimes say to Joy (again, only half-kidding) that left to my own devices I would live in one room, have a few hooks for my clothes, rarely talk, eat chips, and drink beer with the occasional piece of raw meat thrown into my cage.

Of course this is an absurd male fantasy, to which Joy would roll her eyes, remind me that my closet was overcrowded, that I talked too much, and that she would gladly toss raw meat at me from time to time.

When I said something stupid, Joy liked to say, "It's a good thing you're cute!"

I don't want to sugarcoat it. I mean, we were not strangers to the word *divorce*, anyone married for forty years who says that is a liar. Sometimes we meant it, in those heated moments when you're saying the mean things that you shouldn't be saying, and later you're sorry. After a really bad fight and the requisite hours of freeze-out, we'd make up and it was sweet if a little bitter, often tearful on Joy's part, who wasn't a crier but knew how to do it, and it was interesting, even intriguing to wonder where all that anger and animosity went. We talked about that too. Maybe that's why we survived as a couple, because we talked about everything, not right away — we could both be reticent about expressing our feelings, even shy — but we were truthful with each other, knew the other's weak spots and darkest secrets, which became woven into the fabric of our relationship as best they could. Some baggage is lumpier and harder to weave in, but you have to make room for the bad stuff, like a Persian carpet with the necessary imperfection, everyone has one, or two. You don't have to love them, not even like them, but you do have to acknowledge they exist and are part of the deal. On occasion, you hit a snag, sometimes it doesn't feel like anything big, but if you let it grow, like a weed left unattended it can spread and take over your once well-tended garden.

We were twenty-plus-years into our marriage when we hit one of these rough patches, nothing specific, just that we were in a state of constant annoyance with each other, and so we went to a marriage counselor.

I initially feared that the therapist, a woman, would side with my wife and it would be two women against one poor man, or that a woman therapist would undoubtedly think I was an asshole (and sometimes I was), though in fact she often took my side, not that she said I was right (good therapist that she was she never said *anyone* was right — or wrong), but she pointed out how Joy often misheard what I said or misread my actions, not only in the clichéd men are from Mars, women are from Venus way, but in the more specific ways that long-term couples stop listening because they're so used to hearing each other speak they no longer recognize what's actually being said.

The therapist taught us how to fight fair, how to give up the notion of being right (not easy), of calling a truce without harboring resentments (also not easy). I added a statute of limitations because Joy tended to bring up annoying things I'd said weeks or months earlier. The new deal (according to me) was if something was bothering either one of us, we had three days to bring it up or that was it, case closed.

The therapist also helped us see the ways in which we'd grown together and the ways we'd grown apart, and to consider which things still worked for us, and which things needed to be reconsidered. And she gave us homework, about fighting and talking, and it was, in some ways, as if we were a new couple, occasionally awkward, but interesting and ultimately good, as it helped us stay together rather than come apart.

Joy and I hadn't planned on children; Joy always claimed she wasn't interested, and me, the *artiste,* had no time for such things.

That changed when Joy's biological clock started ticking. She turned to me in bed one night and said she wanted to have a baby. I remember saying in my usual flippant way, "Let's not discuss it *here,*" but I considered it and finally said, *Why not?* (There was something exciting, romantic, and narcissistic to think about creating a mini-me.)

Joy was the one to insist we go to Lamaze classes, though the night they showed the film of a woman giving birth she came home, got into bed and said, "I've changed my mind, I'm not having the baby," then pulled the covers over her head and went to sleep for twelve hours.

When Dorie was born, everything changed. Our life as carefree young adults ended (there wasn't time for fighting, fair or otherwise), and going out almost every night, which we had for years, was over. Having a baby pulls you out of your devotion to self; the baby doesn't care if you're a famous artist or a famous anything. It wants caretakers, a mom and a dad, or two moms or two dads, or at least one solid person who will attend to its needs, physical and emotional. It's a big job, and no matter how many books you read (Joy read Dr. Spock and many others; I read none) it is pretty much on-the-job training.

The birth of our daughter begins to play in my mind: Joy's water breaking, waiting the appropriate time before going to the hospital — after midnight on a frigid December night. I see Joy on the curb outside our building half bent over with contractions, and me trying to wave down a cab. Fifteen, twenty minutes pass before one turns the corner. I make a dash but two yuppies in suspenders and topcoats, clearly drunk, appear out of nowhere and beat me to it.

I catch up to them. "My wife is pregnant" — I say, pointing at Joy — "in labor!"

"Go fuck yourself!" one of them says.

"Are you *deaf?* My wife is having a *baby,* you asshole!"

"Ass-hole?" He sputters boozy breath in my face, hand gripping my arm.

I tug free and am ready to throw a punch when I hear Joy shout: "I'm having a *baby* and you're starting a *fight* with those *idiots?*"

The cabdriver gets out, looks at Joy, tells

145

the yuppies to get lost, and helps Joy into the back of the cab, the only sane man among us, Joy thanking him, then muttering at me.

At the hospital, it turns out we have miscalculated and it is a long night before Joy is in full labor, delivery not until the next day, which is, to me, terrifying to behold. I secretly long for the days when fathers paced in the waiting room while their wives went through hell. But then the baby's head appears and her body slips out and it is a *miracle!* The midwife hands me a pair of surgical scissors. "Cut the umbilical cord," she says and when I hesitate says, *"Now!"* and I do it.

A few moments later the baby is cleaned up, wrapped in a blanket, and handed to Joy, who asks me for her glasses — she is blind without her contacts — and I take a photo: mother and child just minutes after birth.

I find the photo in an album Joy had put together of Doria's first month of life. It's small and blurry; my hands were obviously shaking. I know I can do better.

Here's the thing about having a baby: you never talk about anything else! It's why parents of babies need to find other parents of babies — because no one else can bear

to be around them. Joy and I talked about
The Baby constantly. We rebonded over her,
now the most important thing in our life,
and a new chapter for us as a threesome,
not a duo.

An actress friend was the first person,
outside of me, to know Joy was pregnant
(though I don't think she knows it). She
had come to dinner the exact night of Joy's
third month and as she was leaving said
something about babies and why didn't we
have one. She was about to leave when Joy
blurted out — "I'm pregnant!" She turned
around, and she and Joy talked about babies
for an hour. We ended up borrowing a varia-

tion of her sister's name, Dorrie, which became Dorie, which became Doria, "in case she wants to run for president," Joy said.

Our friend was back in California so I wrote to give her the awful news of Joy's death, which I did with several friends who were not geographically close — a lot easier for me than speaking the words. She called immediately, asked how I was doing, then cried out, "But what about *Joy*? My God — poor Joy!" And it struck me that she was absolutely right, that it was Joy who had been cheated. With her first book about to be published and her career flourishing, Joy was entering a period of self-fulfillment, of a return on all of her hard work, and the biggest cheat of all: not being able to watch her daughter grow into the successful young woman she knew she would be.

I can't help but think how Dorie was cheated too, how they were both cheated, mother and daughter. Sometimes I think Dorie's loss is greater than mine. Joy and I had already shared a lifetime, but Dorie's life is still at the beginning, and there is something so primal about losing your mother, so profound and irreplaceable. Not that I think loss is quantifiable, but I know the relationship this mother and daughter had, the deep and limitless love Joy had for Dorie, the hopes and dreams, the pleasure she took from every one of Dorie's successes, the pain she suffered over any and all of her disappointments.

There are times Dorie calls with a question or a problem and I know it's not me she wants to talk to, not my opinion she is seeking, but Joy's, and I try to put myself in Joy's head, try to be Mom rather than Dad, to answer the question as Joy would have, though I'm never sure I get it quite right.

I want to call Dorie now but she's on a job, in Los Angeles. I have a need to talk. I want to tell her about Joy's singing and dancing in the theater group, something I don't think she knows and will enjoy hearing. She's been away for several weeks and I miss her; I've grown accustomed to having her nearby, much more so in the past months than ever before.

I go to her website, peruse her various fashion jobs, then stop on an interview with photos of my fashionable daughter looking very young and very innocent, another photo interview where she looks glamorous.

I don't even think about it. I just start drawing; it has become my way of staying close.

As I draw I think about Dorie, the innocent and the sophisticate, who she was and who she has become, her many attitudes and faces. It's odd, I realize, that I can actually picture other images as I draw. I sketch very quickly but after only a few minutes I decide it's *too* fast, too light, lacking substance, and I decide to do another.

A Dorie memory medley stutters through my mind: playing Mary in the Christmas pageant at school in Rome; high school graduation in the Friends Meeting House; at Skidmore College, graduating with honors, fresh-faced and grown up all at once. I recall one of the snapshots Joy took is framed on the shelf above her desk.

I remember the day as I work: Dorie and her friends, Joy and I watching with pride as Dorie got her diploma, the three of us together afterward, a threesome I took for granted.

In the drawing, there is something not quite right about Dorie's mouth, which I erase and redraw, an improvement, not perfect but a lot better than the photo, with more life.

My eyes hurt. I close them but cannot sleep.

I call Dorie but can't remember if there was a specific reason I had wanted to call. I get her voice mail and simply say I'm call-

ing to say hello. I hang up thinking I forgot to ask how she's doing.

21
PILLS

I am heading down a tunnel of blue-white phosphorescence, ducking in and out of a series of rooms, all empty, bleached of color and life. I pass doctors and nurses, ask each of them if they know the mysterious emergency room doctor. They ignore me. I am about to give up when I go through a door into a small, dimly lit room and there is Joy, looking as she did the very last time I saw her, bruised and lifeless.

I awake with my heart pounding, head throbbing, gasping for breath as if coming up from deep water. It takes a moment to realize I have been dreaming.

It seems to me, and has even been suggested by a doctor friend, that I am suffering from a mild case, or perhaps not so mild case, of PTSD.

Sirens bring back every moment of that day in vivid detail, along with thoughts I cannot stop: Did Joy know what was happening? Was she in pain? Had she been frightened? Of course she was; I saw it on her face and the way she reached out to me.

For months I could not sleep. I could barely close my eyes, my nerves so close to the surface that the slightest noise made my body twitch. For almost a year I could not go anywhere noisy; I walked out of dozens of loud restaurants, had to leave gatherings simply because the talk became deafening, everything amplified as if I were wearing hearing aids turned up too high.

Though I would spend the day exhausted, longing for sleep, when night came it was impossible.

My nighttime ritual, for months, was the same. After hours of overstimulating television, the laptop propped on my chest — my best and worst distraction — I'd pop a pill (or two), but the moment I felt drowsy and closed my eyes the images would swarm into my brain like a SWAT team and I'd drag the laptop back onto my chest for another episode of . . . anything.

It seems — or seemed for a very long time — that the nightmare was always there, waiting for me to fall asleep, my very own Freddy Krueger.

When not glued to my laptop I would lie

awake, in bed, checking the clock every hour. Often still up at 4:00 or 5:00 a.m., I'd finally fall asleep only to slip into one of the recurring dreams I'd have between sleep and waking. . . .

I am in a large empty room, no furniture, no windows, no objects. The walls and floor are transparent. Across the room, and through one of the scrim-like walls, I spy Joy. Through the gauze she looks like a ghost, but when she slides through the wall and is in the room with me, she looks very much alive. The fraction of my mind that is conscious thinks: *But that's not possible.* Neither of us speak, or maybe we do — who can tell in a dream? — either way, there is a palpable tension between us, as if we've had a fight, though it's nonspecific, just a feeling of something *off* between us.

I awake in a foggy purgatory, wondering what is true: *Is Joy alive or dead?* Part of me is truly uncertain, unable to shake the dream. It is another minute before I glance over at Joy's side of the bed and see that it's empty. (For months I would slide under the covers on my side of the bed careful not to disturb her side, which remained perfectly neat.)

In the other recurring dream, I see Joy's face and she is mouthing the words,

Where . . . have . . . you . . . been? She is reaching out for me but I am immobilized, as if attached to some imaginary anchor.

Recently, I've added a new dream to the repertoire.

I am home in the loft and everything seems normal. I spy Joy on the living room couch, reading. I'm startled, but excited. *She's alive!* Then suspicious: *How can she be alive when I know she is not? Is it a trick?* I go into her office and find the box of ashes. I think: *If Joy is alive, then whose ashes are these?*

In the past I never remembered my dreams. Now, I can't forget them. It's as if they are inside me, dormant, waiting for darkness to come alive, to pounce.

For months I stayed awake as long as possible to avoid sleep, to avoid the bad dreams, binge-watching *House of Cards, Breaking Bad, Orange Is the New Black, The Fall, True Detective, Transparent, Californication, Happy Valley, Catastrophe* — Netflix and Amazon could not create the shows fast enough for me. Often I'd look forward to the late-night watching no matter what else I was doing — deciding whether or not it was too early to leave a dinner or an event to get back to my addiction — to not talk, to not think, to be distracted, to be oblivious.

The laptop viewing made it possible for me to be alone in my loft, alone in my bed with a cast of characters to keep me company, a good and bad thing: harmless, though nonproductive; passive, yet over-stimulating — I know the laptop tends to keep me awake rather than lull me to sleep. *One more episode* fast became another mantra.

I should have thrown my laptop away for many reasons, the most obvious, my red itchy eyes, which became a sort of condition that not only drove me crazy, but made me feel as if I were going blind.

I went to three different eye doctors, one referring me to another, "Just to be certain there is no underlying condition."

The third ophthalmologist looks as if he hasn't smiled in a decade, mouth tight and drawn. He has put drops in my eyes and sent me back to the waiting room while my pupils dilate. Now, half-blind, I am back in his examining chair.

"Do you watch a lot of television?" he asks.

"Hardly any," I say. "I watch Netflix or Amazon on my laptop."

"That *is* television," he says with a deep sigh.

"Oh. Right," I say.

"How many hours?"

"Hard to say." No way I am going to tell him half the night.

"How close is the laptop?"

"On my chest."

He sighs again. "With your eyes — near-sighted, astigmatic, plus the fact that your eyes do not work together — watching a lot of television — and it's television whether it's on your laptop or not — is making your eyes work overtime. Do you wear your glasses when you're watching?"

"No. It's the perfect distance for me."

"Wear your glasses!" he says. "Are you on the computer a lot, other than watching television?"

I tell him yes.

"Big screen, or small?"

"Big," I say, convinced I am doing at least one thing right.

He shakes his head. "The eyes have to constantly adjust to different areas of a big screen causing eyestrain. Plus, your tear ducts are clogged. Do you ever cry?"

I am startled by the question.

I see my mother at my father's funeral, Jackie Kennedy stoic, not a single tear.

Like my mother, I could not cry for my wife. I have only once, at the hospital, with Dorie sobbing against my chest, a reaction,

I'd say, to the intensity of my daughter's pain. Now, when I think I might cry, I fight the tears and end up with a headache and red, itchy eyes.

I leave the doctor's office with prescriptions for two new pairs of glasses, one with prisms for up-close work, and a prescription for Restasis, to stimulate my tear ducts. I wear the prism glasses a few times then stop; they give me a headache. The Restasis makes my eyes burn worse than before. I call the doctor. He says to keep going, says that I will get used to it. I force myself to use the drops another two weeks, then toss the expensive, three-month supply in the garbage.

My eyes have become, at least to me, symptomatic and symbolic of what has happened, my tear ducts clogged or dried up, lids red, the one part of me, if you look closely, that gives away my sadness. For the first time in my life I am happy to hide behind my glasses.

Though I give up the Restasis and the prism glasses, I do not give up the laptop on my chest nor any of my nighttime regime: I take lorazepam, my drug of choice, every night, sometimes several times during the night, though each time I tell myself I will soon stop, that it is temporary, and that it is okay because I only take the pills at night.

Tonight, the vial of lorazepam is not in its usual spot on my bedside table. I look under the bed, perhaps it's fallen — no; it could be in the night table drawer, maybe it's rolled in — no again; I go to the bathroom medicine cabinet, though I'm sure I have not put it in here, and I'm right, not there. Soon, I am pushing vitamin jars and bottles of aspirin aside in the cabinet above the kitchen sink, a wave of anxiety prickling my skin. I go through my pockets, anything I've recently worn. I pluck shoes off the floor and shake them upside down. I go through my travel bag — surely there must be a few pills in here, but there are not. Panic is starting to set in, the thought of facing the night without drugs, terrifying. I shake out blankets and sheets.

Then it hits me: I cleaned off my bedside table late last night and tossed out a vial of Ambien because I am convinced the drug makes me more depressed and I did not want to take one by mistake. Perhaps I have thrown out the wrong vial.

In the kitchen, my hands deep in food scraps, old tea bags, and grimy deli wrappers, I find no pills. I dump the garbage onto the floor, and there is the Ambien, two pills left in the vial, which I pocket, just in case. There is no other vial amid the mess on the floor. Still on my knees, I run my hand beneath the kitchen island; my hand comes away greasy. In the bathroom, I rummage through shelves under the bathroom sink and check behind the toilet.

The pills are nowhere.

I sag back against the shower door, and try to think. I can call the doctor and get a new prescription — but not at two in the morning. Plus, it is a controlled substance refilled a week ago; he will not refill it again so soon.

I wonder if I can score tranquilizers on the street? I think about calling my friend who has a pot dealer, maybe he can get me something. But it's too late to call him; too late to call anyone. The Ambien will have to do.

I take the pill. It knocks me out for a few hours, but that's all. The rest of the night I float in an uneasy twilight zone, and the next day I feel awful, not from the realization that I have an addiction, but from the aftereffects of the sleeping pill, which has left me feeling suicidal, and I mean that literally — I think about killing myself on and off all day.

I need to kick the habit. I decide I will

give up lorazepam; I know I can do it. It's a simple question of mind over matter, isn't it? After all, I'm not a junkie. I feel good making this decision. I am on the road to recovery.

That night, still filled with my newfound resolve, I find the vial of lorazepam tucked halfway under the edge of the bedroom hamper, hidden by a runaway sock. I immediately take a pill.

22
WHAT I KNEW

Dorie insists that if I redecorate the bedroom it will help me sleep. I need, she says, "to change the room and make it mine." I have my doubts. I'm not even sure I want the bedroom to be mine, not sure if I am ready to purge Joy's taste and presence from the room.

Dorie suggests a new bedspread and pillowcases to start. "We can deal with painting the walls another time."

She walks me over to Restoration Hardware, where we spend an hour looking at samples. When the young man who has been helping us tells me that the items I have finally chosen have to be ordered and will take two to three weeks, I have a meltdown.

Are you kidding? No way!

Suddenly, the bedroom transformation seems urgent to the point of dire.

Dorie tries to calm me. The salesman

explains that the store no longer stocks anything, that it is too expensive, that everything is made to order, which brings on meltdown number two.

Why did I bother to come here? I've wasted hours. I could have bought everything online. This is absurd, ridiculous. You're not a store — you're a virtual catalog!

The salesman sells me the samples. Clearly, he wants this crazy man out of the store.

I bring the bedspread and pillowcases home. They are a deep brown color, ribbed, and unlike anything I've ever had.

I lay the new bedspread onto the bed and a decorating daydream blooms in my mind: I will paint the walls the color of sand and replicate one of Georgia O'Keeffe's desert paintings for over the bed, or possibly get a long-horned cow skull and a small Navajo rug for the floor!

For a few minutes I am consumed by this Southwest fantasy: I am a cowboy, exchanging my New York costume of black jeans and tees for bolo ties and turquoise bracelets.

Of course I do none of this.

In fact, nothing in the entire loft has changed. Joy's collection of McCoy pots are everywhere: thirty or more on a shelf built specially for them in the living room, more on end tables and window ledges, two lamps on either side of the sofa have been made out of McCoy pots, another twenty or so on a high shelf in the kitchen, a McCoy tea set sits on the kitchen island. Joy started collecting them in the seventies when they were cheap, nothing above twenty dollars. They doubled in price in the nineties (Joy blamed Martha Stewart), and prices have continued to rise, though they are still a relatively inexpensive collectible.

Dorie and I used to kid Joy that one day we'd retire on her McCoy collection. Nowadays, I give them away to any of Joy's friends who want them, and there are still plenty. I don't particularly like them, but they are a symbol, a daily reminder of Joy, and I don't see how I can get rid of them.

Other than the pottery, everything about the loft is spare and simple, a reflection of Joy's taste.

Some days I think this is a bad thing, that it's time the loft reflected *my* taste — some eclectic mix of art by friends, my collection of snow globes and Mexican crosses, African masks, and who knows what else — prison art, thrift shop paintings — and yet, I have changed nothing. The loft remains exactly as Joy left it.

I stare at my new bedspread. I think: Maybe I can at least muster the energy to paint the room some drastically different color other than white.

Black?

There is something mordantly funny about that. It brings me back to when Joy and I first met and I was living in a basement apartment in Boston with three roommates, John, Juan, and Al, and we had the brilliant idea of painting the apartment walls black. Picture it: a basement apartment with three or four slits at ceiling height passing for windows and we painted it black. *Glossy* black. It was like living inside a patent leather shoe. I remember Joy's shock when she first saw it. Later, when we were dating, she insisted she redo my bedroom and she did: the wall behind my bed wallpapered with broad horizontal stripes of mauve and purple, the rest of the walls painted pale lavender. It looked like a whorehouse, but sweet, and I liked it. When I think about it now, it's as if someone other than Joy did the decorating, it was so unlike her. Then I remember she was trying to mimic the pastel prettiness of *The Umbrellas of Cherbourg.*

I come back to the moment and wonder if redecorating will change anything, or if it will simply emphasize the fact that I am trying to erase my wife and will therefore heighten my guilt.

There it is again, guilt, the paralyzing force that prevents me from changing anything in the loft, possibly anything in my life. Even *thinking* about change makes me feel guilty.

Before I settle into bed, I take the new bedspread off, fold it up, and store it away.

I close my eyes and the all too familiar pictures spark in my mind — the paramedics, the race to the hospital, the waiting room. I sit up and reach for my laptop but stop, because I see something else, what I have been trying to see, the needling thought I've suppressed taking shape in my mind like drops of ink in water, spreading like a Rorschach image ready to be decoded.

I see us on the couch, my arms around Joy, her eyes open, hand gripping mine. Then her eyes close, her body sags, her grip eases. I hear the sirens outside, then the buzzer sounds. I let go of Joy and she slumps against my chest. I lean her against the couch and say, "Hold on!" then sprint across the room and press the button to release the front door. I am just getting my arms around her again when the firemen and paramedics charge into the loft and tug me away. I watch them roll Joy onto the floor, tear open her blouse, press her chest up and down before the second team arrives and there is more CPR.

But what I do not see — what I never saw — is any kind of response from my wife, who remains inert and lifeless throughout it all.

The pictures stop playing. I stare into the dark of my bedroom and think: I *knew* this. *Knew* it when I asked the fire chief to tell me Joy would be all right, *knew* it when I paced in the waiting room, *knew* it when I told my daughter that "Mom will be okay," the whole time denying what I *knew,* denying what I'd *seen* because it could not possibly be true — that someone could die in an instant — that my perfectly healthy wife could die *just like that* — because these things do not happen.

But it did happen.

And I saw it.

Before anyone had gotten to Joy, she had died, at home, in my arms.

I did not sleep that night, and pills were no help. This new "information" did not make me feel better, or worse. Did not exonerate me or lessen my guilt. It was simply a fact — a testimony to the hope I held during those excruciating hours in the hospital waiting room, an homage to my denial. It is just another image, or a modification of an old one, something to add to the nightmare reel I have stored in my mind.

I discussed this with my internist, who said I didn't see it because my mind had shut down, because I was in denial or more likely in shock.

It took me a while, but here's what I've come to believe — with grief, you don't know it until you're in it; with shock, you don't know it until you're past it. Often, it's hard to know what is shock and what is grief, where they intersect and overlap, where one ends and the other takes over.

The medical definition of shock describes it as a drop in blood pressure while your heart beats faster, your kidneys working overtime until they eventually shut down.

This is not what I mean. I'm thinking of a more mental, emotional shock, where you are jolted by something terrible — a violent attack, or in this case, a sudden death — something closer to shock therapy, where electricity is jolted through your brain to cause loss of memory, of connective brain tissue, of normal thought patterns and pathways, which is how I felt, though I had no idea for months that I was not myself, that nothing connected or made sense.

When I think about that day, if asked to

describe how I felt, I'd say it was as if I'd been in a terrible accident, that I'd been hit by a truck or a bus and was stunned, paralyzed, beyond physical pain though every part of my body ached and felt leaden, my mind like the white noise machine Joy and I had used in our bedroom for years to blot out the city's cacophony, a buzzing monotone.

I wish someone could have explained to me what I was going through, could have said, *In a few months you will look back on this and see that you were pretty much out of your mind, but you will get better.*

Because I *was* out of my mind.

I don't mean that after a few months I was over my grief, but rather that those first few weeks and months were like nothing I've ever experienced — and I just didn't know how bad I was until I was past it and was able to look back.

23
THE ELECTRIC EEL

Since Joy died I have dropped a heavy wooden painting panel on my foot, which fractured several bones. I have tripped, hit my head on a table, and knocked myself unconscious, awakened seconds or possibly minutes later, with my face in a pool of blood, nose broken and forehead lacerated, which later needed stitches in my eyebrow, and embedded glass taken out of my lip. Not long after that, I slid on wet leaves running to the subway, twisted my foot, and tore ligaments.

There were other, minor accidents, a badly cut finger, another less serious fall. There were two bouts of a serious backache, something I have never had in my entire life, though Joy had a bad back, and suffered semiyearly flare-ups, no matter how much she exercised. I wonder if I have internalized Joy's back issues, and worse, if I am constantly hurting myself or getting sick as some sort of penance.

There are also the continuing eye issues.

And the migraines.

I have always been a headache person. From the time I was a teenager I had headaches. Tension headaches. Cluster headaches. I rarely had, or have, a day without some form of headache, slight to moderate to bad to very bad. At one point, when I was young, I started taking Fiorinal for the bad ones, a drug that worked but pretty much rendered me useless for an entire day. I stopped taking the drug when I learned it was dangerous, plus the cure seemed almost as bad as the pain.

For many years my severe headaches had abated. I'd still have a low-level headache or an occasional bad one, but debilitating Fiorinal headaches had pretty much gone away.

Until Joy died.

It started with a flickering light in front of my eyes. It was late and I was watching TV. At first I thought there was a weird wavy electric line moving across the screen. Then I realized the wavy line was *inside* my eye. It looked like an electric eel slinking across my field of vision. For a moment, I truly thought I was going blind or having a stroke, but the electric eel finished its path and moved out of my vision. A half hour later I was hit with pain, thunderous and nauseating.

I took a bunch of aspirin. The next day I was fine, and decided to forget it. A week or so later, it happened again.

I have always hated going to the doctor and put it off as long as possible. (And without Joy around urging, insisting I go, it was easy.) I rationalized that this new brand of headache had been brought on by a combination of stress and eyestrain, a reasonable and convincing argument.

When I had a third one, I recognized they had a clear pattern.

At first, it's as if there is some sort of obstruction in my vision, a light spot or blind spot in part of my eye. It's a few minutes before I realize it is the onset of the electric lights — or what I've come to call "the eel" — before the actual headache arrives; it is also the moment when I realize there is nothing I can do to stop it, because once the lights start, that's it, there's no turning back.

The fourth time, I am on the New York State Thruway at the beginning of a three-hour drive when the lights start. I try to ignore them for a mile or so, then realize I am essentially driving half-blind. I pull off the road into one of those all-in-one gas stations, and wait for the lights to stop. When they don't I go in and buy a bottle of Advil. I take three. I lean back against the car's headrest, and with my eyes closed watch the electric eel begin its dance on the inside of my optic nerve. Twenty minutes later, when the lights have stopped, I get back on the highway; the migraine doesn't hit for another half hour. When it does, I drive through it.

This is who I am, or at least partially, a man with a high pain threshold.

When I took the fall that lacerated my forehead, broke my nose, and rendered myself unconscious I was staying with friends and it was the middle of the night. Once I came to, I rinsed the blood off my face and got back into bed. I actually slept (something the emergency room doctor, whom I saw the following day, said was the worst thing I could have done; that I could have died). When my friends saw me in the morning they not only shrieked, but immediately took me to the hospital.

My point about this is that I knew I'd done some damage but could bear the pain. And there's something else: I didn't want to be a bother.

I think that ties into the general idea of

not asking for help — not when I've fallen and smashed my face, not when I am grief-stricken. I believe that men are more prone to this sort of behavior, and it's not only a problem but can be foolish and dangerous. I think my father was the model, apparently ignoring the pains in his chest, arm, and legs for months until he had a major heart attack; this, coupled with my mother's constant cheer and never wanting to be an annoyance.

If there is one thing I am trying to learn, it is this: *Ask for help.*

After the road trip headache, I was worried. Many years ago, I'd read Oliver Sacks's book on migraines because it fascinated me. Now, I decided (after some Internet surfing) that I was having migraines and they were no longer fascinating, just terrifying. Would it happen again — and worse, why were they happening at all?

I had one more before I finally went to see my doctor, who immediately sent me to a neurologist. After a battery of tests and questions the neurologist agreed with my self-diagnosis, migraine, though she insisted I have an MRI, "just to be sure," with a look that suggested more.

I'd heard stories about MRIs, about the loud noises and claustrophobia that drive some people mad, not to mention the underlying worry that I might have a brain tumor.

On the day of the MRI I felt strangely calm and when I saw the gigantic MRI machine I laughed: it looked like something from the set of a 1950s Buck Rogers sci-fi movie, outdated and goofy.

Going into the close-fitting tube was like slipping into a spaceship.

Then the noises started. Then they got worse. For a minute, a long minute, I felt panicked. Earlier I had considered a lorazepam but decided against it, not because I was brave but rather because I was afraid daytime pill popping would cut down on the meds' nighttime efficacy, or that I would start taking the pills all the time and not just at night.

When the MRI sounds were just edging on intolerable they started to remind me of something — a Merce Cunningham dance accompanied by the usual bombastic John Cage music. I scanned my memory for Cunningham images and found them. Not so difficult as I had, at one point, made a series of abstract paintings based on Merce Cunningham dances. I locked the images into my mind. For every clang and boom I saw dancers dart across a stage — and it worked.

Afterward, I was filled with a kind of sadness I could not locate until I realized it had been Joy who introduced me to the world of dance and how we never missed a Cunningham performance.

I had to wait a week to get the MRI results. While I waited I imagined my death and realized I did not want to die. For months I had not really cared if I lived or died. Now I cared. There were things I wanted to do. And I had promised my daughter I would not die.

It turned out that I did not have a brain tumor.

The MRI, according to the neurologist, showed that my brain was "normal." I couldn't help but think what Joy would have said if I'd told her that, and the laugh we'd have shared.

24
LOSING AND FINDING

It is late afternoon on a dreary winter day, the sky over Manhattan like a low-hanging slab of slate, the entire city an oppressive gray monochrome, the wind chill factor hovering somewhere around zero. I have taught a class at Pratt in the morning and appeared to anyone who may have been watching as totally normal, in command of my subject, crime writing, my old verbal self, despite what was probably three hours of sleep or less. In just a few more hours I will be going to dinner at the home of my good friends Jane and David, and I look forward to it. They have been the best of friends, inviting me to go out or to their loft for dinner almost every week. They have not let me down.

But right now I am pacing from my studio to the front of my loft and back. I would go out but I don't think the city's frigid temperature and emotional chill will do me any good. There is a specific urgency to my fretting today: I can't sit still because I feel as if I am losing whole pieces of Joy.

For one, I cannot recall her voice.

How is that possible? We lived together for over forty years.

I know I have an old phone machine, disconnected months ago, which I saved because Joy had recorded the outgoing message. I need to hear it but have no idea where I've put it. Sleep-deprived and jittery, my mind racing and scrambled, I go from studio to living room, from junk drawers to file cabinets to closets to stacks of stuff under my studio desk to Joy's office, but cannot find it anywhere.

I look again and again. It has to be here. But where? I hate myself for this, for my slapdash organization, which is no organization at all, something Joy would never do; she could always find anything.

After an hour, fatigue and frustration have gotten to me. I give up, sag onto the paint-stained sofa in my studio, and then it gets worse.

I think: I cannot conjure up Joy's face.

This is absurd. I know her face by heart. I have looked *at* it, *upon* it, *stroked* it, *petted* it, *kissed* it, hundreds and hundreds of times. I know it in repose, I know it smiling, I know it in anger and in sadness.

And yet, I cannot see it.

I close my eyes, but my mind is a blank. I breathe in through my nose and out through my mouth. I tell myself to let my mind go. I press my fingertips against my lids. I sit back. I wait. I continue my self-conscious breathing, and eventually it comes to me, Joy's face, in its many moods and the many phases of her life. It is almost comforting, but not quite. There is something too ephemeral about the pictures in my mind, which come and go quickly. I am still worried I will forget and need to do something more permanent.

Maybe it is time to resurrect the photos.

I retrieve the one I have hidden on the shelf under my studio desk, the one that used to be *on* my desk, a black-and-white photo I took of Joy and Dorie when I was teaching drawing at a small art school in the South of France. Almost immediately, I want to put it back, to hide it away. Instead, I get out my pad and pencils. I put on my earphones.

In the past, I'd fill a large part of my free-flowing unconscious with music. There'd been a time in my life when I said I became an artist so I could listen to music, I loved it so much, but I could no longer listen to music at all, it was simply too emotional. Sad music — my favorite — got under my

179

skin, even the corniest sad song could bring on a wave of depression, while upbeat music made me edgy and nervous, and so I gave up music for over a year — one more loss.

I find a podcast I have listened to before so I will not really have to listen again though it will provide enough white noise to keep me from thinking. I turn the volume down so it is just above a whisper. Now I force myself to look at the photo analytically, to stare at it in fragments. Soon, I am replicating those fragments on paper, and really *seeing* them — the curve of Joy's arm, the beauty of her hands, the waves and curls of her hair — and in so doing, I remember all of those things too.

At some point, I put the photo aside, and just work on the drawing, the graphite lines and marks that represent my wife and daughter at a particular moment in their lives.

I take in the drawing and not only recollect the moment but it comes to life: posing Joy and Dorie just so, *smile, don't smile, look at me, look away,* until they were exasperated and protesting, and I hear Joy's voice! Soft but throaty — *Get on with it!* — and I see the look in her eye directed at me followed by her deep laugh, and it is alive and real, and with it random memories ripple back: Dorie at the beach, Joy the one who

180

played with her in the water (I had to be coaxed; Joy was a great swimmer, I am not); taking Dorie to restaurants even as a toddler (she always behaved), and how she liked to eat almost everything (including sushi!), until she was five or six, when it appeared she ate nothing at all (I remember how Joy and I worried she was starving and referred to her as an "air plant," though the pediatrician assured us she was fine and healthy); then the moment captured in this drawing when Dorie was seven, and once again ate everything. I feel myself smiling as I look at the sketch because I know there is

no way I will forget, not Joy's voice nor her touch, not her scent, nor the freckles on her arms and legs and cheeks, which she did not particularly like, but which I loved.

I look at my drawing and the years blur — time changes dramatically when there is a child growing up in your home — and I wonder if this current period in my life, also a blur but a different kind, will move as quickly, though it seems to drag in the way things do when you are watching, waiting, and hoping for them to change.

25
GOOD AND BAD FRIENDS

The restaurant is an old-fashioned white-tablecloth sort of establishment, most of the tables filled but the place is quiet. I spy my friends, let's call them Joe and Anna, across the room, a nice-looking couple, both impeccably dressed and groomed; *well-heeled* is the word that comes to mind as I head toward their table.

It is the first time I've seen them since Joy's ad hoc memorial, a few weeks earlier, the longest and most difficult weeks of my life, and there had not been a word from either of them until yesterday, a surprise and a disappointment, as they are very close friends and have been for decades.

Yesterday, when Joe finally called, I made a point of saying not to wait for *me* to call or ask for help, that I was incapable of doing so. *Okay!* he said, underscoring the word, *Let's make a date!* We tried but he didn't seem to have any time. They had this engagement or that one, were caught up in various holidays and travel. Only one option was extended. They were meeting a friend from out of town for dinner the following night and perhaps I would like to join them. *No, I would not.* I wanted them to myself, not to be shared with a stranger, but since it was all that was offered I took it.

They stand to greet me, kisses and hugs all around. They already have drinks. I order a glass of wine.

We have planned to meet early, a half hour before their friend's arrival, so we will have time to talk.

So what do we talk about? New York real estate, a recent gala they have attended, this and that. All fine, though I have lost my taste for small talk. Neither one of them asks me how I'm doing or expresses any thoughts or feelings about Joy's death. It is as if nothing at all has happened. Perhaps I am the one who is supposed to bring it up, this ugly topic of death, but can I actually ask them to *ask me* how I'm feeling or coping? A half hour passes. I feel the minutes ticking in an urgent, almost physical way, knowing their friend will soon show up and the opportunity for any real talk will be lost.

Perhaps Joe and Anna think that avoiding talk of Joy's death is better for me, but aren't your good friends supposed to be the ones you can talk to about such things? At least a little? That's all I expected, a few words, a couple of sentences. I did not want to make an evening of it, surely not out in a restaurant. But there is not a word on the subject.

I understand that some people simply cannot deal with death, and that no one knows what to say. (I never did, though I've learned, the hard way.) But one needs to find the words to overcome whatever it is that makes this so difficult. Others had.

By the time their friend arrives I am already so disappointed and depressed that I've got my mask on so tight my jaw hurts and I am developing an earache.

Their friend is nice enough, though I can't remember a word she said other than her inquiry as to how we three had met.

Joe explains how we met decades ago and became good friends. He describes us as "family."

A few weeks before, I would have agreed. But if he believes that now, how to explain their virtual disappearance, their lack of making time for me?

I order a second drink, sit back, and watch the three of them talk and drink and laugh. Joe is the more effusive, as always, and

185

funny. Several times the three of them are laughing and I observe them as if watching a play; nothing strikes me as funny tonight. It is as if they are at one table and I am at another, though I'd say the gap seems larger, like separate planets. Once or twice I feel Anna, who is seated beside me, staring at me, but when I turn to face her she looks away. Is she embarrassed to look at me now, after almost thirty years of friendship? Is she trying to *see* how I feel without asking? Is she searching my face for signs of change? I have no idea. She doesn't say much during dinner, not so unusual, she is the quiet one in the couple, the one who was closer to Joy, though she has not said a word to me about how she has taken the loss.

I say very little too. I feel as if I am on the other side of a one-way mirror; I can see them but they don't see me. I want to leave, but I am paralyzed.

Everything about the dinner seems to be in slow motion, endless. When it's finally finished we are outside on the street, a balmy night, summer fading fast, the three of us alone again, another opportunity to ask me something, anything about my current condition, but again nothing is said. There are brief hugs and talk of seeing one another soon, and I walk the twenty-odd blocks home, just short of running, fueled by a fusion of sadness, pain, and fury. I can't remember another time in my adult life when I have felt more disappointed or hurt by friends I have loved.

It is important to admit that during this period of my life I was oversensitive, often upset, hurt, or furious. Everyday incidents or things people said that I would normally shake off or laugh at now reduced me to quaking rage or sunk me into depression. It was as if a layer of my skin had been peeled away, and I was exposed and vulnerable.

Clearly, Joe and Anna had no idea how I felt. I have asked myself why many times, and I think I was at least partially to blame. I've already said how I put on a mask, how I rarely if ever asked anything of anyone. Most friends saw through it, but others, like Joe and Anna, apparently bought my act.

The dinner was more significant for the way *I* acted, which is that I did not act at all, and it's important that one *must* act, must get up and leave. Forget other people's feelings. This is *your* time to feel bad, your time to protect yourself — but I did not.

A week or so passed and I couldn't take it. I e-mailed to say I wanted to talk, but did not say why. I wanted to air my disappointment, wanted to fix it, wanted to love them again. Joe e-mailed back: *I have a little time between a meeting and my trainer, maybe a half hour.* No alternatives were offered. I dropped the idea of the talk.

A few more weeks passed.

An e-mail invitation came: Would I like to join them for dinner in celebration of a mutual friend's birthday? To me, the message was clear: they did not want to see me alone. I declined.

Perhaps they thought I needed or wanted space, and so they gave it to me.

Perhaps they thought I pushed them away, though I'd acted with them exactly as I acted with any of my friends, most of whom called and stayed in touch, asked me how I felt and told me how they felt, made time to see me, frequently invited me out or over to their apartments, and came through in one way or another.

More than a month passed before another invitation was extended, this one to have dinner at their apartment. Finally. It felt too late but I accepted. I had, by this time, relegated them to a lesser category of friend, though I wasn't ready to cut them out of my life. They still meant a lot to me, still reminded me of so many good times shared with Joy, and I harbored some hope of reclaiming the friendship.

I arrived thinking I would tell them how much they had disappointed and hurt me, but actually doing it, confronting them in person, was impossible. For months, I'd been working overtime to keep myself together and confrontation of any kind was out of the question, I simply could not handle it.

It was a pleasant enough evening, just the three of us, and the old friendship was there on the surface. I think I did a good impersonation of my former self with perhaps even more forced good cheer than usual.

I did not have the strength to confront them that night or any other night. Time passed, too much time. My anger toward them turned to a kind of apathy. Now it's hard to take them back. They failed me as friends, but I failed them too. I've relocated them to the outer fringes of my life, and it's clear they have relocated me as well, though it still hurts and haunts me. It remains one of my biggest regrets, a loss within my worst year of loss.

So how does one begin to repair or forgive people who were simply not there in your darkest hours of need? The answer, I think, is to not let it happen in the first place, not to let things go that long before saying *something*.

More than a year after Joy's death I will read a riveting and beautiful book, *The Iceberg,* by Marion Coutts, about her husband's battle with brain cancer. Throughout her husband's illness, Coutts sent group e-mails to friends and family not only as updates but to remind them to stay in touch, to visit, to help babysit her toddler son, even to deliver meals. I found this amazing. Something I could not do, nor even consider doing.

But why not?

I'd say because I was so deep in my cloud of despair and working so hard not to appear so, that it simply never occurred to me. Of course my circumstances were very different from Coutts's. The shock of unexpected loss was paralyzing for me. I could never determine the *correct* way to let people know how I was feeling or even if I should; it somehow felt too private, or even wrong, to air my feelings and needs.

I question if this has something to do not just with my personality, but with the more basic genetic fact that I'm a man.

I know Joy and I would have discussed this particular situation endlessly — *Do you believe Joe and Anna have been completely AWOL? What do you suppose is going on with them?* I also know that Joy would not have confronted them; she was even less confrontational than I am. Perhaps it's not just a question of gender, but I wonder if Joe and Anna would have acted differently toward Joy if *I* had died?

Looking back, I see that my emotions were totally out of whack, though I'm not sure that excuses friends who did not make the effort to try to understand what I was going through. The fact is, losing one's partner is an unsolicited litmus test. Some friends pass the test beautifully and others fail.

26
THANKSGIVING

The end of summer and early days of fall seemed to drag on forever. Then suddenly it was Thanksgiving, Joy's favorite holiday (once we'd disentangled it from family and adopted it as our own, which we had for the past decade or more). The new Thanksgiving consisted of our nuclear family, Joy's sister, Kathy, and husband, Charlie, always Jane O'Keefe with some of her family and friends, along with good friends orphaned from their families. It became a great tradition and something we looked forward to every year.

Joy would cook up a storm, a rarity, but she did it well. She'd order Indian corn from a company out west (creamy and delicious), brine and braise the organic turkey, make my mother's cranberry mold (the one and only carryover from my childhood Thanksgiving), bake her two best desserts, a plain orange pound cake just for me because I loved it, while everyone else devoured her rich and decadent Chocolate Bruno. People would bring vegetable dishes and apple pies and lots of wine and Jane would make the gravy and we'd argue every year that mine was better (though it wasn't). I'd make stuffing and watch the same video every Thanksgiving about the best way to carve a turkey, and it was a great holiday, no religious overtones, no father turned away from the table to watch the football game, no childhood angst, no endless drive on the Long Island Expressway, no after-meal headache from anxiety. Joy's Thanksgiving — and it was very much hers — was a glorious event, and anyone who came begged to come back.

Joy insisted on a sit-down meal, never a buffet, no matter how many people. I ended up building an extension for our table, as it grew from ten to twelve to sixteen to eighteen people.

So what do you do with a holiday when the person to whom it mattered most is no longer around?

You ignore it.

And that's what Dorie and I did.

The idea of going to any other Thanksgiving, at anyone else's home, was impossible. When Thanksgiving rolled around, just three months after Joy died, the two of us left town.

That first year we flew to Arizona, spent one night with my oldest childhood friend and his beautiful Lebanese wife, who cooked a delicious Middle Eastern meal for a dozen though we were only five.

The next day Dorie and I take off in our rented car, a Jeep, since we have planned some long-distance and heavy-duty driving, though we start out on the normal tourist route. First, Sonoma, where we buy rocks and crystals (many related to grief, the smooth black Apache Tears, my favorite, one I continue to carry in my pocket). Then, to the Grand Canyon, which Dorie has never seen. We have reserved a cabin only yards from the canyon, too dark to see when we arrive, though we awaken to a startling view, then hike a few miles along the rim.

We both know it's something Joy would never do, that she hated heights and would be freaked to see her husband, and particularly her daughter, sitting on the edge, posing for pictures, soft rocks crumbling under our shoes and rippling down into the canyon.

It is the first of several times we are able to talk about Joy, even joke about her. The jokes get more extreme when I drive up

Mesa Verde to see the Anasazi Indian ruins, hairpin curves that would have had Joy weeping, and I'm not kidding. Years ago, we were driving south on California State Route 1, the high winding coastline between San Francisco and Los Angeles, past Big Sur and Point Lobos, beautiful and breathtaking, *if* you're looking. Joy was not. She was half under the dashboard, *crying.* She finally begged me to head inland, and I did, through artichoke farms and small towns, an interesting, if lackluster, route that took us hours longer and was something I teased her about for years.

I think about that ride now as our Jeep climbs up the mesa's icy road. It had snowed only days before, something we had not anticipated: that it would be cold in the Southwest.

"Oh my God, if Mom were here," Dorie says, reading my mind.

"We wouldn't be doing this if she were," I say, and it's true, though clearly Joy's ghost is with us. I keep hearing her say, *Turn back — stop — be careful, you've got my daughter in the car!*

It's easier to joke about what Joy would or would not say or do, but not so easy to get past the jokes to something real. I'm still not ready. If Dorie is, she doesn't say.

Throughout the trip, Joy's ghost continues along for the ride and we are happy to have her though I am conscious of not saying too much because I don't want to ruin our good time. I still see it as my *job,* my fatherly *duty* to protect my daughter's feelings, whether she wants me to or not.

I see us driving through the desert, as Joy and I had done so many years earlier, and I think of radio talk, this time Dorie an equal partner in the talking marathon. But we do not talk much about Joy, or our feelings about her, or what we have been going through, not in any substantial way.

I finally abort the treacherous drive up Mesa Verde a quarter mile from the top. Joy was right; it *is* too dangerous — one skid and we'd be goners. I find a small place to turn around and Dorie and I hold our breath as we wind our way back down to flat ground.

On Thanksgiving Day we drive into Flagstaff and everything is closed, no one on the streets, a ghost town. At the one open gas station I ask if there is any place in town to eat. The gas jockey tells me, "It's Thanksgiving, a *big* holiday," as if I am a foreigner or new to the planet, then adds, "There's one place, Josephine's, but you'll never get in, people make reservations a year in advance."

Not one to be deterred, I find the restaurant, the parking lot full, people dressed up for the day crowding the entrance.

As soon as I spot the maître d', a young guy and good-looking, I position my beautiful daughter in front of me, drop back a few feet, and she gets the message. I can't hear what she says to the guy (though I watch her body language change), and a minute later we are ushered to a table for two. The food is surprisingly good, a Thanksgiving buffet, delicious and copious and we eat a lot, so much so that we are too full for dessert.

I am almost, but not quite, surprised when the young maître d' follows us out to the parking lot with desserts he has personally wrapped and hands them to Dorie, along with his cell phone number.

That night, after a four-hour drive with lots of radio talk and many laughs, we stay in a shabby motel on a Navajo reservation, where we eat tinned foie gras that Dorie has brought from home, smeared on crackers, and drink good red wine bought in Scottsdale, and talk about how Joy would have hated the motel and how miserable she'd be if she were here.

Dorie brings up Joy's unfinished book and I discuss the trouble I've had finding a good independent editor and the fact that I have already fired two: the one Joy had hired to assist her, who became overwhelmed after Joy's death, then myself, whom the publisher encouraged to do the work, but as I could not be objective and had little knowledge of the subject I was a disaster. Lately, I too have been feeling overwhelmed and out of my element, and more than a little worried I have taken on a project I will be unable to finish. Of course I tell Dorie it will be *fine.*

I'm taken by surprise when she asks if I've had any luck obtaining the autopsy results. I tell her no and she gets annoyed.

"Why *not*?" she asks.

I explain the red tape I've been dealing with and she sighs. I feel her frustration and agree, though it feels as if her frustration is not with the system but with me.

"Don't you want to *know*?" she asks, plaintive and irritated.

"Of course," I say. "And I will."

Then we are both quiet. Dorie has turned away, and is writing in a notepad, though she doesn't reveal what she is writing. I try to read a book, impossible.

We are sharing a room in the shabby

motel and I feel the absence of Joy's presence in an almost physical way. I wonder if Dorie feels it too, though I don't ask.

The next day we are the lone couple in Canyon de Chelly, on horseback, freezing our asses off as the only Navajo guide we have been able to locate and rouse leads us deeper and deeper into the frigid canyon, stopping to point out petroglyphs as our horses splash through half-frozen streams and I grip the saddle horn with gloveless hands, my fingers going numb. An hour and a half in, we tell the guide we've had enough, but it's another hour and a half back until we can huddle in our rental Jeep, hands and feet under the blasting heater, the two of us practically crying, our appendages prickling with pain as they defrost. I'm not sure, but it feels as if we have come dangerously close to frostbite.

Once again I hear Joy: *What have you done to my daughter!*

On the last day, we are in Albuquerque, New Mexico, both exhausted, tired of traveling and sightseeing, when Dorie says, "Let's go to a movie." We find a nearby twelve-plex and go into the next available movie, something with Jennifer Aniston, about a family road trip and drugs, a perfect midday escape, and it strikes me that there

199

are very few people (other than Joy) who would forgo the possible pleasures of Albuquerque for a less than mediocre movie, but Dorie and I are in sync, and we not only like the movie, but are relieved to no longer be sightseeing.

The trip is locked in my memory as *fun,* possibly the only fun I had in those first months, even the first year, and it was a surprise, because Dorie and I were still reeling from shock.

On the day of Joy's memorial, a close friend, a retired therapist, someone I have known since college, had come in from Mexico, where she lives, to be with me for a few days. At one point, she said I should try to think of something good that could come out of this tragedy. At the time I was shocked by her question — how could I dare think of something good? — but I thought for a moment and said, "I can watch *American Horror Story,* Joy wouldn't let it into the loft, it was too scary for her." A flip response, though my friend's question stayed with me and every so often I would try to come up with an answer. Now, after these Thanksgiving trips I have one: I can spend as much time with my daughter as I like and not account for it to Joy, who often felt left out when Dorie and I were together.

The triangle created in only-child families is difficult and inevitable — someone is going to be left out, and it's not going to be the child, who has known, since infancy, how to get his or her parents' attention, even if it means separating them. There were plenty of times I was the odd man out, but I didn't mind. Joy did. Though incredibly close, she and Dorie had some of the typical mother-daughter angst. Dorie and I had none — at least I don't think so. Dorie and I also share a similar sense of humor that drifts toward the ridiculous, something Joy never quite got. I picture the three of us at dinner, me and Dorie convulsed with laughter and Joy just sitting there. Even now, it makes me laugh.

I am thinking all of this as Dorie and I exit the movie theater and head into the parking lot. I have my arm around Dorie's shoulder and she is leaning into me, tired or perhaps melancholy, though I don't ask which.

The Thanksgiving escape has become a tradition, one I would like to think will go on forever. Of course nothing goes on forever. I know my daughter will eventually create her own Thanksgivings with her own family, a good thing and I hope so, and not be traveling with her old man.

The second trip — I am skipping ahead — was to Istanbul, and it was particularly good to be out of the country, where Thanksgiving was just another day.

The most recent trip was to Mexico City, and it is on this trip, despite the fun, and there is lots of it — great meals, great Frida and Diego art, great walks, and more — that I feel some tension between us, feel that Dorie is annoyed with me, sometimes losing patience.

It erupts after a wrestling match in a huge Mexico City arena — something everyone should see for its high camp and performative value, the incredibly acrobatic wrestlers in garish costumes pummeling one another, the entire audience hooting and shrieking and whistling along with the grating sound of noisemakers, an audience of mostly young couples and Mexican families with children, all making an unbelievable racket. And yet there is nothing that compares to the two teenage girls seated directly behind us, who are *shrieking* and *screaming* non-stop, and at such a high pitch and intense volume that it is unlike anything I have ever heard before, beyond deafening, my ears throbbing, and I soon have a headache, a bad one. I want to throttle the teens, but tell myself it is their event, their way of having fun, I am the foreigner, the intruder, they are just having a good time.

But I am not. And I can't take it for very long. After an hour that seems like three my head is exploding and I would not be surprised to see blood leaking from my ears.

I tell Dorie I have to leave. She sighs and shrugs. I'm not sure if she wants to stay, though frankly I don't care; I have to get out.

I stop at the men's room and Dorie heads outside though I have asked her to wait. It's a while before I locate her and she's angry, arms locked across her chest, lips pursed. We are in the middle of nowhere, and it's a seedy part of town. We have apparently missed the Uber car she's called, somehow my fault, though I didn't know she'd called one. We have been Ubering all over the city for a week, it's been cheap and easy, and now, sighing, Dorie Ubers another. We wait. Nothing. Dorie is pacing. She texts the driver, who says he is here. But where? We can't find him. We are traipsing up and down the dodgy street in front of the arena, Dorie striding ahead of me, seemingly in a rage. I don't think I have committed any sort of cardinal sin, but I've apparently done something. She is still angry when we get into the car. I ask what's wrong. She shakes her head and sighs.

It's not a big fight, not really a fight at all. It feels as if there is a wheel slightly askew and it has thrown the cart of our relationship just slightly off-kilter.

It is our last night in Mexico City, it's late, and we are tired. We go back to our rented apartment and do not say a word about it. Not yet. I take a bunch of aspirin and get into bed. I feel an undercurrent of something brewing, something important, as if I've missed an opportunity with my daughter, but I'm too tired to talk. One more time, I store my feelings away, one more time I avoid the conversation we need to have, the one that is coming.

27
LILY

Beside Joy's main closet is a tall stack of shelves where her sweaters and tees are neatly stacked. I kept this door closed, but every morning it was open. For a while I thought the magnets that held the door in place must have weakened, or it was some weird settling of the building, though I couldn't remember it ever happening before. Every night I closed it. Every morning it was open.

It started to feel eerie.

Then, one morning, still in bed, I saw the door bang open, and Joy's cat, Lily, jumped out. When I investigated I saw that she had made a sort of nest on one of the shelves among Joy's sweaters by rumpling them up, and she'd obviously been doing it for some time, the imprint of her body along with a thick pelt of cat fur made that clear. Did she actually wait for me to fall asleep each night, then manage to open the door to sleep among Joy's clothes, to inhale her scent, to be with her? The next night I waited and watched closely as the cat quietly pawed the door open and climbed in. How had I missed it before?

Joy always said that when she got very old she wanted to have dozens of cats. Though she never got very old she did have several cats, though not at the same time.

I'd grown up with a dog I adored, a golden cocker spaniel, Mr. Cosmo Topper, just plain Topper for short, but Joy converted me to cats. We each adopted one in college; I got Beads, Joy got Lulu, and we had them when we married. The two cats became inseparable friends. Beads was gone many years before Dorie was born, and Lulu had the intelligence and good graces to bow out at eighteen only a few months after our baby was born.

We let our daughter, at a very young age, choose a scrawny ugly kitten from a local shelter. I had tried to influence her to choose another, but while a shelter volunteer fetched the pretty cat, the ugly one was put into Dorie's arms and that sealed the deal.

My daughter named her Brenda, after a character on *Beverly Hills, 90210*. She turned out to be a hisser, a scratcher, and an occasional biter. Not what we had in mind for our six-year-old daughter.

And so Lily, a beautiful calico, shy and scared, was adopted as well. Brenda, by default, became my cat (no one else liked her). Lily, though intended for Dorie, in actuality became Joy's cat, and they adored each other.

Brenda mellowed with age and I grew to love her. She died at twenty-one, in good health and good shape up until the last months of her life. In the end, a vet came to the house and put her to sleep in my arms, something I would like when my time comes.

Lily didn't seem to notice that Brenda was gone; they'd never had much to do with each other. She remained as close to Joy as ever, if not closer, following her around and avoiding me.

After Joy's sudden death, Lily's dislike for me escalated. Most days she hid under the bed, nights she inhabited Joy's closet or the living room, as far away from me as possible. If I came too close, she bolted. If I tried to touch her, she hissed. I doubled my efforts to befriend her. I fed her extra cat food, which she whisked out of her bowl onto the floor where it was left uneaten for me to clean up. I bought her toys and treats, all ignored.

Then the howling began. Several times a night I'd come out of the bedroom to find her in front of the elevator that serves as our front door, performing a doleful aria — piercing, hollow, mournful, and very, very loud. Clearly, she was waiting for her beloved mistress to come home.

Her howling was like the crying I could not do.

I begged her to stop. "You're killing me," I said.

These intense howl-fests went on for months, a late-night opera to accompany my insomnia.

Then, six months after Joy died, I was invited to Yaddo, the venerable arts colony in upstate New York, where I had been several times over the years, a place I love, which has rescued me more than once. Yaddo had always been the perfect place to think and work away from the disruptions of regular life. But now, I wasn't sure about going. My New York life was not only disrupted, it was completely disjunctive and disconnected, hardly a life at all. I barely slept. I had not worked. I hated being home but was afraid to leave. Dorie said, "Go, it will be good for you." Yaddo's president encouraged me, as did the program director, who said, "Yaddo is a healing place. You should come." Their words touched me, but I was still unsure as to whether or not I could actually go. I had a million excuses why I could not.

And there was the question of Lily. No pets are allowed at Yaddo. But how could I leave her alone for three weeks? And with whom? She hated everyone and was scared of everything.

I broached the subject with the colony staff. I explained that Lily was old, declawed, and would probably hide the entire time. She was granted special dispensation, like a Seeing Eye dog or in this case, a grief cat, and so we went, Lily howling and shaking as I put her into her cage, me equally nervous about leaving home alone for the first time since Joy had died.

A half hour from home I felt lighter, an actual physical feeling, as if a literal weight — one that had been crushing me — had been lifted off my body.

We arrived at Yaddo at night, the place quiet, beautiful, Gothic and mysterious as ever. If you didn't know, you might have thought it was uninhabited.

I brought Lily inside my Yaddo digs and opened her cage, but she would not come out, frozen, unmoving. I spoke to her in hushed tones trying to coax her, but it wasn't until later that night that she ventured out, looked around, and made a beeline for the back room, where she hid under the bed. I put out her food. A day passed. The food was uneaten.

Another day passed, more food left uneaten. I started to worry.

The next morning half the cat food was gone, though Lily was back under the bed and no amount of coaxing could get her out.

Meanwhile, I was acclimating. It was strange to be away, but familiar too, the colony a place I had always gone alone, without Joy, and so it was easier than I had anticipated. I felt no less sad but better than I had in months, able to breathe, and after two days, able to write, which I had been unable to do at home. I was thankful to be there.

In the late afternoon of the third day Lily emerged from under the bed, let out a howl, and let me pick her up. She didn't squirm or hiss. After a minute she started to purr. She rubbed against me, even licked my arm, a first, and a shock. "It's you and me, Lily," I said. "We're all we've got." She looked at me sleepy-lidded, purred, and pressed closer. We stayed that way for almost an hour. I suggested to her, aloud, that since she was at an arts colony, she write a book of poems.

After dinner, I returned to my rooms and Lily greeted me with another cry, a familiar one she had used with Joy, one that meant "pet me," and I did, ending with her curled in the crook of my arm where she fell asleep and so did I. She stayed like that all night.

The next day was the same but even more intense. She wanted to be near me, on me, paws kneading my chest, purring loudly, drooling onto my shirt, often licking my cheek or the tip of my nose. Sometimes she'd spend fifteen minutes diligently washing my arm. Every night she slept with me. This was the routine for my entire stay at the colony.

So what happened? What miracle occurred that made the cat not only accept me, but adore me? Was it being away from home? Was she scared? Or was it simply time? Maybe she finally came to her senses and realized *He's as good as I'm going to get.*

Back home, Lily and I remain as close as we'd been at Yaddo. She still howls, but it is reserved for evenings when she wants me to get into bed and pay attention to her.

She curls up with me every night, and I hope Joy is watching. I think she would find

it incredible, though heartening, and it makes me feel as if I am doing at least one thing right.

While at Yaddo I made several quick sketches of Lily. Back home, I made a more finished drawing.

Lily is eighteen and though healthy, I know she is aging out in cat years. I worry that losing her will bring about a new round of mourning not just for her, but because she is a direct link to Joy.

For now, having Lily purring beside me

on insomniac nights may not exactly fill the void, but her living, breathing presence provides comfort. I look at her and think she obviously decided to make the best of things; she moved on from one person (Joy) to another (me), a progression we all have to figure out sooner or later.

28
CLEANING OUT THE CLOSETS

It was almost a year before I cleaned out Lily's nest and finally managed to deal with Joy's clothes. I wouldn't have done either, but it was a matter of practicality; I was going off to two different writing residencies, had given my loft to friends, and needed to make closet space for them. Otherwise, I'm pretty sure the clothes would still be hanging in the closets and Lily would be curled among the sweaters.

I told my daughter it was time. For months she'd been saying she wanted to be there when I did it, but kept finding reasons to put it off and I'd go along with her until I no longer could.

We set a date.

When the day came, I didn't want to do it but held firm.

I called Dress for Success but they turned me down; they only wanted suits — *Really? In today's world?* — and Joy did not wear suits. She wore sweaters and slacks — in a couple of sizes, depending on her weight. (Like many men, I was in the constant no-win situation of "Honey, does this make me look fat?" If I said no, Joy said, "You're not really looking at me." If I said yes, which I never would, I was a dead man.)

I thought about this now, almost smiling, as I arranged for a charity in East Harlem to pick up her clothes.

Dorie arrives. She has already done this job upstate where Joy had kept her summer and gardening clothes, a chore Dorie and I started together, but soon overwhelmed I'd needed a break. I told Dorie to wait until I got back and we'd finish together, then I took a ride and did a few mindless errands. By the time I returned there were several large trash bags filled and ready, all of Joy's clothes packed, Dorie's face puffy from tears.

"I didn't want you to do it," she said.

"But honey . . ." was all I said. I wanted to say, *But she was your mother and this is just as bad for you.* But she already knew that.

She was taking care of me. But who, I worried, was taking care of her?

Now, in my Manhattan bedroom, Dorie

and I attack the job. I shut my emotions down as best I can and work on automatic, unlike Dorie, who is very much in the moment, going through every one of Joy's items carefully — sweaters, blouses, T-shirts, shoes, bags — considering each piece and choosing what she wants to keep. Joy was not a clotheshorse though she always looked good in her cardigan sweaters (there are dozens and dozens of them) and white tees and white blouses and low-heeled shoes.

I am inside Joy's closet when I hear Dorie say, "What's this?"

She is on Joy's side of the bed emptying a drawer, and when I look over she is holding a stack of letters.

"These were at the bottom of the drawer," she says, "and they're from you."

I stop what I am doing and join her.

The envelopes, faded white, legal size, are bound together by an old rubber band.

I see Joy's Boston address on the top one, and recognize my handwriting, a lot neater and better forty years ago than it is now. I start to slide the rubber band off and it breaks. The letters fall to floor and scatter, all to Joy from me.

Dorie stares at them a moment, then helps me pick them up.

"What are they?" she asks as I open one.

"They're from me," I say, "written to Mom when she was in Boston and I was in graduate school at Pratt, the year before we were married."

"Love letters?" Dorie asks.

I unfold a letter, written in longhand, and read it to myself.

My darling Joy,

School is intense, but I love it. I'm living in a one-room studio apartment on Washington Street just a few blocks from the Pratt campus. It's got a hot plate, a half-fridge, and a shared bathroom in the hall, bare bones and pretty awful but I'm happy to be here. I stapled fabric over one wall where the plaster was badly cracked and Beads likes to climb it and hang from the top near the ceiling like a gargoyle. It's funny. You'll see when you visit next month.

I picture the apartment, Beads hanging from the wall. I stop reading and say, "sort of," in answer to Dorie's question. There is something embarrassing about reading letters I wrote forty years ago, and I don't want to read further.

"Are they all from when you were in grad school?" Dorie asks.

I thumb through the letters and nod, then sag onto the bed Joy and I shared for forty years, grasping the letters in my hand. All around me are stacks of her clothes — heavy with her perfume, Joy by Jean Patou.

I fold the letter back into its envelope.

"Aren't you going to read them?"

"Not right now," I say.

I get up, find a new rubber band in the kitchen, and wrap it around the stack of letters. I'm not sure where to put them.

"You're not going to throw them out, are you?"

"Of course not."

A quiet moment passes.

"Mom saved your love letters," Dorie says, almost to herself. Then: "Did you save hers?"

I tell her I did not.

This is when she says, "You are the most unsentimental man ever."

I use the excuse that men do not save love letters. But maybe some do. And I wish I had. I'd have read them now. I had no idea Joy had saved mine. It was a complete shock, touching and sad.

I put them into the bottom drawer of my bedside table. I don't think I will ever read them, they're my words after all, but if Joy could keep them for forty years I will keep them too.

Eventually, we fill nine extra large Hefty bags with clothes and accessories. The process is even worse than I imagined. It feels like a betrayal — *You are giving away my clothes, you are erasing me!* — and it makes the reality of the loss too real. I feel sick, alternately chilled or feverish.

But we have done it.

When we finish, Dorie moves the bags into the guest room so I will not have to look at them until they are picked up. Again, she is taking care of me.

I drive Dorie home with the things she has chosen, quite a lot. If she could have taken everything, I think she would have.

She texts me a little while later: I am wearing mom's short boots. It feels good.

That night, I cannot sleep at all.

I watch two episodes of *Breaking Bad* followed by the 1950s musical *There's No Business Like Show Business,* a favorite of Dorie's when she was a kid. I'm not sure if it's the movie's corny family reunion ending, or if it has transported me back to some nostalgic moment with my daughter, but it makes me cry.

The bedroom feels cold and desolate. I worry Lily will freak out if she goes into Joy's shelves and discovers that her nest is gone. I should have left it for her, but by the time I was working on the closet I wasn't thinking, or trying not to.

I feel guilty, not about the cat but about giving Joy's clothes away. I keep thinking I will go in to the guest room, unpack the bags of clothes, and put everything back as it was. It reminds me of the time Joy convinced me to give my sets of Dickens and Twain to Dorie's school book fair, which I did, then bought them back.

I don't think Joy would have any trouble giving my clothes away. She was always more efficient and never a pack rat, often invoking her father's maxim: *When in doubt, throw it out.*

I am the opposite: When in doubt, I keep it.

I lie in bed thinking it would be better to have done the closets earlier, while I was still in a fog of grief. Several friends offered to help, even said they'd do it for me, but I couldn't let them. And yet, a part of me thinks it would have been a good idea. There's no need to go through this. It's too sad. There is simply no way to do this chore without feeling like you are obliterating your loved one. Or, not to think that one day someone will be going through *your* clothes, deciding what to save, what to donate, and what to toss out.

It makes me think, why buy clothes at all? Why buy *anything*?

I roll over in bed. I turn on the bedside lamp. I stare across at Joy's closets, which are closed, but picture the empty interior, the bare hangers.

Would it be better to hire someone to do this, a stranger who could do it without pain and probably do a better job?

Right now, in the middle of the night, I'd say yes.

And yet, I *needed* to be the one to do it. Not that the act provided closure. It did not. I'm not even sure I believe in "closure." But had I relegated the job to someone else, I would have missed the emotion of personally going through Joy's things, which brought back memories, not all of them bad or sad. And I would have missed the letters.

The very next day I go through my own closet and toss out a third of my clothes. It helps to equal things out. A little. It also says: *These are only clothes — not the person* — something I need to emphasize to myself. It underscores the fact that throwing out my clothes does not diminish me, so that clearing out Joy's did not diminish her.

For several weeks I could not open Joy's

closets. Then I did.

It was several months later that I was finally able to move a few of my things into Joy's closet without feeling as if I were invading her territory, or that I had cleared out her clothes to make room for my own.

But even if that were true, is it wrong? I mean, what else is one supposed to do with an empty closet?

For a while, I thought this was the worst chore. But there were still other things to be done, and one particular date that loomed ominously.

29
THE FIRST ANNIVERSARY

I felt the first-year anniversary coming for months in the way one feels any noteworthy event, but this one was tinged with dread.

Dorie and I made a plan to be at our upstate house, but other than that there was no plan; we just knew we wanted to be together.

As it drew near, the dread set in like the onset of flu. I had a headache for days, not so unusual, but my shoulders and neck ached, and I felt jumpy, my nerves on edge. I kept wondering, worrying what the day would feel like, if I were ready and what I should do, what plans I should make, though I didn't make any.

The anniversary fell on a weekend.

That Friday, Dorie and I drive upstate. We talk of our week, our work, and the fact that I have recently hired lawyers to expedite our will, stalled in surrogate court, a complication I do not quite understand, but necessary if I want to (finally) become the heir to mine and Joy's estate — even more necessary if I want the results of Joy's autopsy, which I have been trying to get for a year. It seems absurd that I have resorted to lawyers, but the hospital has been giving me the runaround (a runaround that will continue for almost another year, something that will frustrate and baffle the lawyers almost as much as it does me, something that will eventually come down to a stunning and startling revelation).

Dorie says, "If *you* had died and the hospital had been stalling, Mom would have hired lawyers a *long* time ago."

I am mildly insulted, but it's true. Joy was more directed, able to see things through in ways that have stopped me. I would often ask her to make business calls or follow through on something I couldn't face.

As we travel up the Taconic State Parkway to our country home, the one thing Dorie and I do *not* talk about is why we are going, or what we are "celebrating," both of us exhausted by the time we get there, from not talking about what we need to talk about. We go immediately to bed, though I am awake most of the night listening to crickets and a hooting owl, sounds I have always found soothing, but they do not soothe me now.

Joy and I had bought the house on a whim ten years earlier when we'd been visiting friends on New Year's Day and they told us about friends of theirs who had inherited a house they didn't want, a house that came with an odd caveat: the former owners, a deceased artist and writer, had made a provision that it should be sold to another artist or writer.

Even though we qualified, I did not want a house. Joy had always wanted a place in the country, but we could never afford one. Still, we went to take a look. It turned out to be an old farmhouse, built in 1860, on six-plus acres of land with beautiful old trees, everything wildly overgrown and gone to seed. We couldn't get inside, but peering through the windows we could see years of accumulated mess, hoarder style.

"It has so much potential," Joy said.

I didn't see it, or didn't want to see it, afraid of the commitment.

Joy insisted we take another look, and we did, the next day, this time with the new owners, who let us in. Beyond the interior mess, Joy pointed out the wide-plank wooden floors, the steep staircase with its thick wooden railing, the deep closets, the old-fashioned windows with views of trees and lawn and evergreens, all glittering under a lacy veil of snow.

It was hard to resist Joy's enthusiasm.

The next thing I knew, we'd bought it. Along with a thirty-year mortgage.

The house became a combination of good times and financial stress, though Joy adored it and I grew to love the slow, quiet escape it offered from our steady diet of New York City life.

We worked on the house every weekend, stripping floors and painting walls, clearing land and planting grass, mostly by ourselves so that we would come back to the city more exhausted than I can ever remember, muscles aching, but we loved every minute of the work. It was something that brought us together again. Joy, it turned out, was a natural gardener, and I liked it too, despite two cases of Lyme disease. The house was never a showplace, but it was simple and sturdy, with good karma, a phrase I rarely if ever use, but it was true, the house had an aura of well-being.

Dorie was married there, under large tents, on a magical night, even if the magic didn't hold for the marriage.

Joy and I spent whole summers there, often taking walks and drives after dinner just to look at the landscape and take in the rural beauty. Sometimes we talked a lot, sometimes we were just together, and that was enough. It was a quiet, peaceful togetherness and we were happy there.

I think about this as I lie in bed on the one-year anniversary of Joy's death, when the house feels hollow and the sounds of the country night are no longer comforting, the place forever in my mind as *Joy's house.* Without her, I feel like a trespasser, her presence in every inch of this house we worked on together.

I try to sleep but can't. I sit up and turn on the bedside lamp. It casts eerie shadows on the walls Joy and I painted. It's then I decide to sell the house.

And I do, just a month later, against everyone's advice and the cliché of not making any big decisions for a year or more. And just like the cliché I will come to regret it. Not because I need a second home — *Who does?* — but I miss the comforting notion that I can escape the city when the crowds and noise get to me, as they do now, more so than ever.

The next day, Dorie and I hardly speak of the anniversary though, for me, the dread is still there, as well as a nagging conflict:

Shouldn't I be making plans to honor the day, to honor Joy, or is it better to *not* make plans, to treat it as just another day? But is that even possible? I don't know how Dorie feels, she hasn't said.

This time I don't think the lack of discussion is my fault or anyone's fault — we just don't know how to think about the day or what to do about it.

Still, having Dorie with me is a great comfort. I feel smart to have had a child, or perhaps the word is *smug.* All I know is that I couldn't have gotten through the year without her. She was and is, despite any unspoken tension between us, my bright light in a dark season, one of those people with a big personality, someone who attracts others, smart and funny and talented. I can (almost) look at her objectively, and have at times glimpsed her from afar and seen her as a glorious, completely separate human being from myself.

At some point during the day of the first anniversary, Dorie and I light a candle. I'd had it in the back of my mind to buy a Yahrzeit candle, only because I wanted something that would burn all day and I'd seen Yahrzeit candles often enough in my life. My mother lit ones for her brother and parents, and for my father; not that she's religious, but it was something she'd seen her parents do. I'm not religious either, but have a spiritual side (more now than before), one I've often tried to tamp down.

Of course I forgot to buy the Yahrzeit candle, and finding one in Dutchess County was impossible. I consider driving to the other side of the river, to the Catskills, where there are plenty of Jews, but Dorie nixes that idea, as it will take up half the day. I have several candles I'd bought when I was researching Santeria for a novel, covered in decals of skulls and saints, but they are clearly wrong. Finally, we find a tall, elegant, off-white candle, something I'm certain Joy had bought, which we light, close our eyes, and have our private thoughts, and that is pretty much it.

This momentous day, which I have dreaded, turns out to be underwhelming, though sad.

That night, Jane O'Keefe joins us for a quiet dinner on the porch. It is a soft, warm night, pleasant though layered with melancholy. Jane raises her glass of scotch in a toast to her good friend Joy, and Dorie and I raise our wineglasses along with her. It is an odd moment. I cannot say what Dorie is feeling, but I feel a combination of sad and muddled; I can't get my mind around it.

Once again, the person everyone is thinking about is missing.

The three of us clink glasses. The air on the porch seems to still. I look over at Dorie and see that her eyes are filling with tears. I change the subject, say something about the hummingbird that has just skittered past.

The next day I feel disappointed and a little guilty because I haven't done enough to honor my wife's memory, though she is on my mind and in the air in a way that is palpable, her absence almost as strong as her presence.

What I wish I had done: Once again, I am looking back and in hindsight there is clarity one rarely has in the moment, particularly an emotional moment. I think I should have planned out the day and the night, made the anniversary *mean* something, exchange quiet personal grief and reflection for a small celebration with close friends and family (the memorial in our loft remains mostly a blur, and in no way a celebration). The problem is one does not get a second chance to celebrate a date that has passed, but do I really want to add that to my list of regrets? Better to say that Dorie and I shared the day and did the best we could, and that's the truth. It could and should be a new mantra for grief: *You are doing the best you can.*

What I hope for and look forward to now is a bigger, better event, the publication of Joy's book, a celebration of her achievement, rather than her passing, though nudging Joy's book toward publication has been like pushing the proverbial boulder up a hill. The newly hired editor is good but there is so much to do. I have also hired a fact-checker and someone to reconstruct lost footnotes (a big and very serious job; without the footnotes I have been told there will be no book), a photo editor, and more. There have been many moments when it has looked as if no matter what we do, no matter how hard we try, no matter how many editors we hire, Joy's book is *not* going to be published.

Joy's sister, Kathy, has spent hours reading and proofing, not to mention providing an ear and a shoulder when I need them, and a consistent voice of calm (after so many years I have really gotten to see how these two sisters share a unique levelheaded poise). Dorie will soon create an amazingly successful Kickstarter campaign to raise money for all of those aforementioned editorial experts. But right now, at the first anniversary, Joy's book is far from finished and its prospects for publication are not

231

looking good. Every time we get the boulder halfway up the hill it rolls back, or another boulder appears out of nowhere. That late-night promise I made to get the book published "no matter what" is beginning to feel foolhardy, boastful, and increasingly unrealistic.

With the first anniversary behind me, the closets cleaned out, the sweet afterglow of that first Thanksgiving trip with Dorie lingering, the lawyers working hard to push my will through the courts, one might say I was moving forward. And I was. Though the nightmares continued, along with my addiction to tranquilizers, and despite insights into grief and loss, which taught me plenty about life but more about death, the fact that Joy died still felt as unreal to me as it had in those first few days, and I was no closer to believing it or accepting it. Had someone asked me then if I would ever feel like my old self — if I'd be able to shed my mask, get over my guilt, and move past my loss — I'd have said no.

■ ■ ■ ■

PART III
THE WIDOWER

■ ■ ■ ■

30
A SINGLE MAN

I am meeting our friend Sara, a single woman and a successful film producer, for dinner. Racing all day, to teach at Pratt in Brooklyn and back, a meeting uptown, home to change, I arrive twenty minutes late. (In the past I was always on time, but I no longer wear a watch — I took it off the day Joy died and haven't put it back on.)

For months after Joy died I went out to dinner almost every night. Nighttime was, and remained, the worst time, and though I was in a constant state of exhaustion from not sleeping, I could not stay home. Though I'd done a large percentage of the cooking during our marriage, I could not cook now, not for one. It didn't seem worth it, nor could I muster the energy. Some people need time to be alone with their grief. I needed to get out.

The Upper West Side restaurant is only half-full, not trendy, with a bit of old-world glamour, red leather banquettes, soft lighting.

Sara, already waiting in a booth, looks up.

"Guess what I've been doing?" she asks.

"Waiting," I say and start to apologize for being late but Sara cuts me off.

"I've been making a list of what I need to do." She has a pad in front of her and begins to read from it. "One: have sex. Two: go away for a romantic weekend and have more sex. Three . . ."

I no longer remember what three, four, five, and six were specifically, but they were very much like one and two.

I am drawing pictures in my mind of *Kama Sutra*–like coupling.

"Oh," I say, trying to keep my cool, but what I am thinking is: I have known Sara for several years and this is the first time she has ever spoken to me in such an overtly sexual way. Is it because I am suddenly available or am I reading something into what is a funny, and innocent, monologue?

I know I am seen differently now. I am, surprisingly, *eligible.* All sorts of friends, and friends of friends, and wives of friends, and girlfriends of friends, want to fix me up with *their* friends. This has to be an indication of the man shortage. Clearly, the criteria — for men — are low. I'm not putting myself down. I know I'm okay-looking and compared to many men my age look better. I walk, I talk, I still have (most of) my hair and all my teeth, I'm not fat, though I've gained ten pounds from eating out almost every night since Joy's death (something Joy would take delight in). I know women are judged more harshly than men, and I also know that there is a shortage of men my age, particularly for women my age.

The restaurant's lights dim, as if someone is watching, trying to add mood to the moment, but it triggers a vision of twilight in my bedroom, and me sitting upright in bed after a bad dream.

I offer Sara a somewhat strained smile.

Maybe, I think, she is just being funny. Because she *is* funny. And we're friends. Not great, longtime friends, but friends. Maybe that's worse: if we were longtime friends the idea of suddenly starting a sexual relationship would be disconcerting, like having sex with your sister. (The idea of having sex with some of my longtime women friends has crossed my mind, though I immediately reject the thought as not only a bad idea, but potentially embarrassing. Plus, I do not want to lose them as friends, and the cliché that sex changes everything is a cliché for a good reason.)

I order a drink. We chat about this and that for a few minutes, now competing with the low murmur of voices as the restaurant fills up.

Sara describes her bad day, which ends with a dialogue about desperate women and how *any* man could easily fuck them. Not exactly a compliment — *if* it's directed at me. But why would she describe herself as a *desperate* woman? She is bright, attractive, funny, ironic, an original thinker, a great character for sure, someone I have always enjoyed knowing.

I think: Am I making too much of it? Perhaps I am the one with the dirty mind.

I think: Sara knew my wife but she knows me better, but do we really know each other at all?

I think: I was never interested in Sara sexually, but then I was married. Do I feel differently about her now?

I think: No.

I think: Did Sara ever come on to me when I was married? *Is* she coming on to me now, or have I been out of the game so long I can't have a woman sexually banter with me without thinking she wants to have sex?

I think: I am thinking too much.

I order another drink.

The room has become noisy, a mix of voices, music, the clang and clatter of silverware, not just annoying but uncomfortable, as we have to lean closer to be heard. I can smell her perfume, something spicy and sweet.

Dinner comes. And goes.

I pick up the check because it has been sitting on the table so long it's embarrassing. Usually, with women friends, we split the check, or take turns buying each other dinner. This time it's clear she is not making a move for the check. I don't mind, except that it makes it feel more like a date.

After dinner, we decide to walk. It is a beautiful evening, one of those sparkling fall nights Woody Allen has captured so well in his romantic tributes to the city. We stroll along the edge of Central Park. Sara loops her arm through mine, not unusual, most of my women friends do this and I like it. In Europe, I see men walking arm in arm, and I think that's fine too. But tonight, after all that sex talk, it makes me a little uneasy.

Sara suggests we stop for an after-dinner drink.

The bar, which has low tin ceilings and mirrored walls, is even noisier than the restaurant, and I can't wait to leave. I down my brandy in two gulps. She sips her bourbon Manhattan and we try to talk over the din, almost impossible. When the check comes she pays. Okay, we're even. Sort of.

We reach her apartment building, large and prewar, cool light spilling from the lobby, her pale skin cast almost blue. She asks if I'd like to come up for coffee. I say no, I have to get up early in the morning. Which is true, though I think of a *Seinfeld* episode, George blathering on about turning down just such an invitation, to "come up for coffee," which he says always means sex.

An awkward moment is followed by yet another invitation — a book reading the following week. I don't say yes or no. I say good night. I walk to the subway feeling a little bad, but mostly confused.

I wonder if I have totally misread the evening.

I wonder if I am being unfair to this perfectly nice, warm, funny woman.

I wonder if I could have gotten laid. I wonder if I *wanted* to get laid.

I wonder if I can no longer be friends with women because my status has changed and therefore anything I say or do can be misconstrued as some sort of come-on when I don't want it to be.

I wonder if I can no longer flirt.

I have become much more aware of sexual tension whenever I'm alone with a woman, any woman, something I did not necessarily feel when I was married.

It all feels very, very complicated. I'm just not used to my new "single man" status.

So what to make of all that sex talk at dinner?

There was a time when I liked overt come-ons (if that's what this was), but I'd say that was between the ages of fifteen and seventeen, when I rarely got them. But now, not so much.

Am I hung up on some out-of-date idea of men taking the lead, of being the aggressor? I don't think that's it.

I have always liked women. Smart women. Funny women. Independent women. (My wife was all of those things — except funny.)

I like women who like being women.

I like women who, despite the fact that it is still, in some ways, a man's world, enjoy being a woman and know there is power in being a woman.

I like women who, though justifiably angry at men for a variety of reasons, understand that sometimes it's not so easy being a man.

I like women who flirt. I like men who flirt too. I like people who feel sexual without feeling predatory. I'm not saying my dinner companion was predatory, just that the conversation made me uncomfortable.

I hear all the time that unlike a widower of a certain age, a widow of a certain age does not get fixed up on dates or invited to parties. A close woman friend of mine, always a beauty and still one at close to seventy, recently told me that since her husband died, almost twenty years ago, she can count on one hand the times anyone has fixed her up or invited her to an event as a single woman. She has a full life, many friends, a good career, and continues to grow as a human being. The only thing lacking in her life is a significant other, not that she wants one full time. She has said as much to me. Is that why she doesn't have one or is it that there aren't enough men to go around? Or not the kind of men she'd like? This is a woman who has had big, important men in her life. To settle for a schlemiel at this point would be difficult, even impossible. (I feel the same way; my wife's low-heeled sensible shoes would be hard to fill.) On the other hand, I know a woman who at fifty-something had never been married, met a man several years younger, they married, and at present are living happily ever after. But still, it's a complicated game, and one I have been out of for a long time.

If one has lived in a relationship for decades, as I have, there are reasons for it. Suddenly finding yourself single is not necessarily liberating since you didn't ask for it or want it. Sex surely fills a moment of loneliness, among other things, but it's tricky, and regardless of the situation, I'd like to think I am at least coauthoring any decision about sex.

31
I'm Just Not Ready — or Am I?

My friend Jenny, successful and social, kept inviting me to her dinner parties. The first invitation came only three weeks after Joy died, way too soon. The next was a month or so later. Still too soon.

Though I went out to dinner with friends, the idea of a dinner *party,* of making smart and amusing small talk with strangers, was overwhelming and just felt wrong.

I declined another invitation until I felt I could no longer turn her down without insulting her, and thought why not give it a chance, give *myself* a chance.

When the day of the dinner party arrived, I almost canceled but didn't. It's not my way; once I've agreed to something I always show up.

With no one around to tell me how I look I waste a lot of time changing my clothes. I have a confession: I was one of those boys whose mother laid out his clothes (from elementary school through high school!). In college, I pretty much wore the same thing — jeans and a T-shirt in warm weather, jeans and a sweater in winter. When I got married my wife didn't choose my clothes, but she had a lot to say about them. Nowadays, I rely on my daughter, the fashion stylist, for advice. (In truly desperate how-to-dress moments I take a cell phone picture of what I'm wearing, send it to her, and she re-plies with a thumbs-up or down.)

Tonight, I text Dorie a few pictures, different shirts, ties. I have decided to dress up more than usual, and it feels good. A shirt and a tie (something I wear maybe three times a year), a vest, and a sports jacket, which all sounds fancier than it is; I still wear black jeans.

When I get there I am way overdressed, the only man wearing a tie, and the Greenwich Village apartment is stifling; I am instantly sweating in my multilayers. The jacket comes off, the tie is loosened.

I don't know any of the guests other than Jenny and her boyfriend.

Jenny, by the way, is a widow who lost her husband to a long-term illness several years earlier. After Joy's death, we met and talked a bit about how I was feeling, which was not at all the way she'd felt after her husband died. Jenny is, by nature, a sweet upbeat person, who had gone through several years of hell by the time her husband died, and so her loss, she admitted, was leavened with a bit of relief.

The dinner party is an impressive group: a newspaper editor, the head of a world-famous auction house, a well-known columnist and his boyfriend, also a writer. It is the kind of dinner party I have enjoyed in the past — smart people, smart conversation. But I'm not sure I'm up to it — everything feels so trivial to me these days, conversation difficult to follow, my mind drifting or going blank.

There is one single woman, a forty-something blonde, very attractive, who, after cocktails, is seated directly opposite me at the dinner table. It doesn't take much to figure out that she's been paired with me, and if so, it's flattering — she is younger than I, intelligent and very pretty.

It is also obvious that she knows a lot about me: that I was an artist, had a fire, have published novels. I figure she has Googled me, or the hostess has filled her in.

Dinner is pleasant. The woman and I have several conversations across the table. She is smart and easy to talk to, though something in my brain, in my grief-addled psyche, stops my thoughts from going any further. Plus, a part of me is self-conscious and a little uncomfortable, watching myself talk to her, considering everything I say before saying it. As soon as dessert is over I am anxious to get going but she is the first to leave. Has she figured out I am a bad prospect and not worth her attention?

We say good night, no numbers exchanged.

I am ready to leave too but have been pulled into a conversation with the auction house guy.

Only a few minutes into it, Jenny signals me from the hallway with a wave. I excuse myself from the table to join her.

"Look," she whispers, displaying her cell phone and a text.

It says something like *You're right, he's sexy,* and something else I no longer remember, because believe me, it's not that often I read a text from an attractive woman that says I'm sexy. I'm flattered, a little embarrassed too, standing there in the hallway, six or eight feet from the dining room table where the remaining guests are still talking and drinking.

"So, you're going to ask her out, aren't you?"

It takes a moment for Jenny's question to find its way into the part of my brain that deciphers language before I say, "I don't think so."

"Why not?" she asks.

"I'm just not ready."

"Go out for a drink," she says. "What's one drink?"

At this moment, a little more than three months after Joy has died, the idea of asking a woman out for a drink feels monumental. I repeat that it's too soon. I think that Jenny, who is not only intelligent but has gone through her own loss, should know that it is too soon for me, despite her good intentions — and I have no doubt that's what they are. I tell her it is not a great thing to do to her friend, because even if I asked her out I am not looking for a relationship, so why waste her time? I repeat, "I'm just not ready."

Jenny shrugs, sighs, a resolved smile.

The next day the blonde from the dinner party sends me an e-mail with a specific question attached, something we have talked about at dinner, though clearly it's an excuse to be in touch, and again, I'm flattered. I answer the question. I entertain the idea of asking her out for a drink. I imagine it as a scene from a movie like *When*

Harry Met Sally, because I just can't imagine it in reality. When she e-mails again, I don't respond. I feel bad. I liked her. But it seems worse to start something that I have no intention of finishing.

For a long time I hear nothing.

A few months later I get a text from Jenny, something like, *I am having coffee with guess who and we are talking about you.*

I honestly have no idea who *guess who* is. Then I do.

I wait a moment to text back. I say something noncommittal like *Say hello.* There are a few more texts but they peter out.

For a few days I consider having that drink again but never act on it. When I think back to our dinner conversations, it seems obvious to me that she is interested in a relationship — not necessarily with me, but with someone — and I am not.

So what do I want?

In the time since Joy died I have given this quite a bit of thought.

I do not want to get married again, and I am not looking for a serious relationship. Unlike some men who need to reattach quickly because they are helpless or can't stand to be alone, I like to be alone and was lucky enough to have had the kind of relationship, the kind of wife, who gave me space. Once, many years ago, at an artist retreat, a woman said, "Your wife keeps you on a very long leash," to which I answered, "My wife doesn't keep me on any sort of leash." I think it was exactly this kind of freedom that made our marriage work.

I recall a conversation Joy and I had about someone we knew, someone whose longtime husband had died and who, a year later, remarried. I was surprised. Joy wasn't. She said, "If you were happily married once, it makes sense that you would want to get married again."

I was happily married, but I do not want to marry again. Though just about everyone I say this to refuses to believe me, waves it off, or patronizes me. "Oh, sure" — "We'll see" — "Until the right one comes along" are the most common responses, all of them usually accompanied by a nod or an eye roll, as if they know something about my future that I do not.

Of course they could be right.

Before I cleaned out Joy's closets I had opened them only once. A good friend of hers was visiting from Paris; it had gotten cold and she needed a jacket.

Michele had called from Paris many times after Joy died. After a few months she insisted she come to see me. As the time drew near I worried about having someone, anyone, around for ten days. I didn't think I could handle my facade of good cheer for that long and in such close quarters. I also worried about something else: I had always been attracted to Michele. Joy knew this and shrugged it off as inevitable; it is impossible *not* to be attracted to Michele, who is not only adorable — and French — but sweet and kind.

Michele was the ideal guest, out most of the day, home for dinner, there in the morning (looking very cute in her PJs), always in a good mood, a sunny presence at a time when there was little sun in my life.

Did the attraction go away? To be honest, it intensified, though I did not act upon it. I'm pretty sure Michele would have been horrified (she has a serious longtime boyfriend in Paris, whom I know), and I would have been horrified too. It's a Hollywood cliché, isn't it, the recent widower suddenly smitten with his dead wife's good friend, one who's come to visit and see how he's coping? I could write the script in my sleep. I knew when Michele was coming that I was in a needy state, how easy it would have been — and was, in a way — to fall in love with her. And I did, a little. Perhaps "love" is a bit strong; "infatuation" is more like it.

After a few days it normalized and was just nice to have a woman around, though it makes me wonder about my resolve to spend the rest of my life alone.

Of course that was ten days. I think I could handle quite a few people for ten days. And this was a lovely woman I have known for more than twenty years, someone I am already comfortable with, even if our situation had altered radically — the person who had brought us together no longer there, though she was omnipresent.

Michele and I spent many evenings talking (often about Joy; Michele encouraged me to talk about her), drinking wine, even laughing, and I missed her when she left.

So, who knows? Maybe I'm just not ready.

32
STUPID THINGS SAID
BY SMART PEOPLE

I am in a Chelsea restaurant, a neighborhood place, seated in a booth. Across from me is a couple I have known for many years. It is a second marriage for both, now married twenty-plus years and devoted to each other. So far the evening has been pleasant and distracting — these are two funny, smart, and accomplished people.

Midway through dinner I tell them that a friend in common, one they know much better than I, has been insistent in trying to fix me up with *her* friend.

It turns out they know the friend's friend.

"She's pretty," the wife says.

"And sexy," the husband adds.

"I'm not ready to date," I say.

The wife waves a dismissive hand. "Oh please, in a few months you'll be dating her or fucking her or fucking someone else for sure." She laughs.

I do not. I am surprised by her statement.

Not for any prudish reason, but for her rather dismissive, insensitive response.

In the past I would have made a joke, now I simply say, "I don't think so."

"Fine," she says — and that does it.

I lean forward and say very quietly but seriously, "I want you to imagine that — — — (I name her husband, who is sitting beside her) has died and it is only four or five months later. Will you be dating or fucking someone else *for sure*?" I surprise myself; confrontation is not my style.

She glares at me, lips pursed. A moment of poisonous silence, which I do not fill.

I file her comment under stupid things said by smart people.

There were so many. But I wonder: Are widows — only months after their husbands have died — told they will be fucking someone else *for sure*? I think not. Though perhaps they would like the option. With men, it seems, everyone is telling you to go out and get laid, though I suspect that when you do, people will talk about you, and not in a nice way.

The husband finally breaks the silence by saying he has no intention of dying.

Over dessert, the wife attempts an apology.

"It was a compliment," she says. "I mean,

you're a catch. You're good-looking and women like you. And there are a shortage of men, you know, decent men, and I'm sure Joy wouldn't expect you to be celibate."

I tell her I don't intend to be, but that it's too early for me to be dating.

Then she does it again, waves that dismissive hand, and laughs. "Oh, *please,* I'm sure you will remarry in no time."

I give her a look and she says, "Sorry, but I just don't see you being unattached for very long."

"On the other hand," the husband says, "why not play the field? There are plenty of single women. You might as well have fun."

The wife glares at him. "That's not what I'm suggesting."

"But why shouldn't he have some fun?"

"He should," she says, "but I think he's the marrying kind. It's obvious, isn't it? He was married for forty years."

"I know," says the husband. "Which is why I think he should play around for a while."

"Play around?" The wife gives her husband the pursed-lipped look she gave me earlier.

"I just think it would be good for him," the husband says.

"Oh, *really*?" says the wife. "Maybe that's what *you* want. People usually suggest

255

things they want for themselves." She bangs her cup down on the table; coffee sloshes over the rim.

"I was suggesting it for *Jonny!*" the husband says.

"Let's just forget it," the wife says.

"Fine," says the husband.

"Fine," says the wife.

A full minute of silence. This time it falls to me to break the ice.

"I'm sure ———— was just thinking of me," I say to the wife about her husband.

But why am I trying to fix their fight? Because I can't stand an angry silence. Because I always want everything to be okay.

The wife turns to me, and hisses, "Well, I hope you *do* play around and fuck a hundred women and tell my husband *all* about it so he can get the vicarious thrills he is so obviously missing."

"Jesus," the husband says.

A perverse part of me is starting to enjoy this, that my situation — the death of my wife, the possibility of my future relationships, the possibility of me "fucking a hundred women" — has *them* fighting.

The wife turns to me again. "Do anything you want. I mean that seriously — *anything.* Have affairs. Travel the world."

Perhaps it's she who wants the fantasy of

affairs and travel, but I don't dare say so.

Later, when I write about this in my notebook, it offers some insight into why newly single men and women are not always welcomed by couples — because they can stir something up, because they represent a theoretical threat: the idea that the newly single can do anything they want, something some couples obviously feel they cannot, something that threatens the basic notion of coupledom.

Did I ever feel this way? *Well, sure.* There were plenty of times I wanted total freedom, not just the freedom Joy gave me, which was a lot. But I've learned something — I've learned that this theoretical freedom is pretty much a fantasy, and I've learned something else: freedom can be lonely.

Another interchange, this one brief, with a neighbor, in front of my lobby mailboxes, uncalled for and unprovoked by me.

"At least your wife avoided a late-in-life divorce," the woman says while casually collecting her mail.

"*Excuse* me," I say, unable to mask my shock to a woman I have seen on a regular basis coming in and out of my loft building for well over a year since Joy has died, someone who has never before said a word about Joy's death nor offered any condolence.

She goes on: "I have several friends in their sixties who are going through divorces, and it's just awful."

You mean, worse than a partner's sudden death? — the thought in my mind commingled with — She *must be worried about a late-in-life divorce.*

I look at her for a moment, then say, "You realize that's an outrageous comment."

"But it's true!" she says.

Which is true? That my wife avoided a possible divorce (though we were not planning one) by dying — or that a few of this woman's friends are going through divorces, which she appears to think is worse than dying? Either way, what does this have to do with me?

One more time I have to say it: Losing your partner is a litmus test. It brings out the best and the worst in people; it provokes good, bad, and unpredictable behavior. I have seen it make people sad, scared, and incredibly insensitive. Odd, that at the moment when you are at your most vulnerable, you are subjected to other people's fears and *their* vulnerabilities.

Here's the thing: Everyone thinks they

know what you want, because everyone thinks what *they* want is what *you* want. I've had countless conversations with friends who tell me what I need to do — sell my loft, travel the world, move to a new city, start dating and/or remarry.

Most people mean well or mean no harm. Yet, my notebook is filled with anecdotes of surprising and (in retrospect) sometimes hilariously bad behavior.

33
WHAT MEN WANT

"What you need is to get laid."

I look across at my dinner companion, who has just spoken that line, a super-successful businessman in a chalk-striped suit, someone I have known for many years. Good-looking, smart, funny, and in personality and profession totally unlike me or most of my other close male friends.

This is the first time I have seen Evan since Joy's ad hoc memorial, about four months ago. Not unusual. He lives on the West Coast and we only see each other a few times a year.

I watch him across the table, his easy smile, the way he sniffs his wine before he takes a sip. I imagine how I would draw him, the sharp planes of his face, his features. Though I have played this role of artist/observer before in my life, of late it has become a bit of an obsession; often I am not listening to someone's words but observing them, their expression, their body language. There is some irony in this as my last two novels featured a police sketch artist who had (supposedly) studied with the renowned facial recognition expert Dr. Paul Ekman, whose system I researched for the book and found fascinating. I tried it myself and was not very good at it, though it seems to have taken root more recently. Perhaps I needed to be quiet, to fold into myself, to stop talking all the time.

"Are you listening?" Evan asks.

"Oh, sorry," I say. "Those women are so loud I didn't hear you." I angle my chin toward the table of women at our right, a convenient excuse as they are all laughing very loudly.

Evan shoots them a glance, half-annoyed, half-lady-killer. "The blonde is hot," he says.

We are sitting at a table almost dead center in an Upper East Side restaurant, the kind of place I rarely frequent, with overpriced food and overpriced people.

"So," he says. "Trust me. You *do.*"

I don't know what he is referring to. I have lost the thread. I try to piece together what he means but can't, something that happens quite a bit these days.

"It will make you feel better," he says.

Now I remember. *Getting laid.*

"You have to take care of yourself, you know. Are you sleeping?"

His concern touches me; I actually feel tears gathering behind my lids. Lately any act of kindness makes me well up, though I do not cry.

"Not much," I say.

He frowns, a deep crease between his eyebrows. "A man's wife dies and he goes to pot. I've seen it happen. Are you eating?"

I nod.

"Healthy food or crap? Don't get fat! It's bad for you and it's not going to help with the ladies." He grins, then frowns again. "You look sad."

"I *am* sad."

"Well, sure. But —" He aims a finger at me. "Sadness is not good for you. It can make you sick."

I tell him I'm okay.

"You know . . ." He looks toward the ceiling, reflecting a moment. "It just could be the greatest pickup line ever: *My wife died.*"

I stare at him.

"Think about it," he says. "The women are going to want to *fuck* the sadness out of you!"

For a moment I am stunned. Then I stutter an involuntary laugh. I have heard many inappropriate comments in my life, and way

262

too many the last couple of months, but this is clearly the winner.

"It's not like when you get divorced, like me, and all the women *know* you're on the make," he says. "Your wife dies and the women want to take *care* of you. I bet they're already coming on to you, am I right?"

Before I can answer he says, "Wait —" tugs a small laptop from his briefcase, types for a minute, then turns it around and sets it up like a mini theater.

The screen flashes a cornucopia of half-naked women.

"Best call girl website out there," he says. "The girls are checked out by the members and rated on a scale of one to ten — are they as pretty as their pictures, are they clean? I'm a member."

"Really?" I am genuinely surprised.

"I don't want to waste my money on girls who don't know what they're doing," he says. "The men are rated too, by the girls, so it's all transparent."

"You've been rated?"

"Yeah, and I got high marks." He grins, a sly wolf. "That way, the girls know you're not a serial killer or a loser or a creep."

"Aren't you afraid someone you know will see you're on the site?"

"Hey, if they do, it means they're on the site too, so what are they going to say? Anyway, I use an alias," which he tells me, way too close to his real identity, if you ask me.

He swipes his finger and picture after picture of seminude women flicker across the screen.

At the table to our right the women have stopped laughing. I can see at least two of them are staring directly at the laptop.

I indicate this to my friend.

"Who cares?" he says and continues to swipe, his vintage Rolex glinting in the screen's sharp light. He stops on one girl after another. "Who do you like — Asian women? Black women? Blondes?" The images skitter by, a dizzying zoetrope of women. He stops at one, a thin, heavily tattooed blonde with enhanced breasts, sitting half-naked atop a motorcycle. "I fucked her," he says, "and she was great. But I'm not going to see her again because the last time I think she was high, and you can't trust a girl who's using drugs. You like her?"

"Not my type," I say, uncomfortably aware of the fact that half the restaurant is watching us.

"You don't like blondes?"

"I do. Sure. Why not? I just think she's

cheap-looking." I feel myself being drawn in.

"I think she's hot," he says, swipes again, and stops at a striking black woman. "I don't know this girl, but the girl I was fucking — the one *you* think is *cheap* — they're friends, and she says she's great." He scrolls down. "Her reviews are great too, all nines and tens. Interested?"

I tell him I don't think I'm ready.

"They've got *pills* for ready," he says with a grin.

"That's not what I meant." I feel as if I am in a movie.

The waiter interrupts. He wants to tell us the specials.

My friend shuts the laptop.

I order pasta. Evan orders a salad. He is watching his weight, though he is as thin and taut as a piano wire. "Gotta look good for the girls."

I think: Do hookers care if you're fat? Aren't they supposed to say you're perfect, no matter what? But I don't say anything.

As soon as the waiter leaves, Evan opens the laptop again and swipes. He tells me about a recently divorced friend of his, "a real toad, but rich, he's got women coming and going twenty-four seven, lucky son of a bitch."

He stops at another girl, this one dark-haired and thin with a smattering of tattoos, wrist, ankle, above a breast.

"Fucked her too," he says, his wolfish grin widening.

"So you like the cheap girls," I say.

He looks hurt, sucks in his lower lip, and closes the laptop.

Why did I say that? Why did I say *anything*? Is this conversation really happening? It feels unreal or real in a reality TV sort of way.

I'm happy when the food arrives.

The restaurant has gone back to its usual hubbub, no one interested in two men discussing travel or the insane state of the world. It quiets again when we finish eating and he pops the laptop open. He taps and swipes, taps and swipes, another array of scantily dressed women dancing across the screen. He stops at a woman with dark almond eyes, caramel-colored skin, long black hair.

"She your type?"

I tell him I don't really have a type.

"But not *cheap*," he says, throwing me a good-natured wink while tapping his laptop screen to bring up smaller photos of the almond-eyed woman at the bottom of her page, these more explicit. He uses his fingers to enlarge one after another, face, breasts, vagina, which has been manicured into a perfect triangle. I tell him it reminds me of a story by the writer Michael Connelly, "The Perfect Triangle," which the author wrote for an anthology that I put together with a friend.

Evan gives me a disappointing look, as though I am not taking the subject at hand seriously. I tell him I'm not a fan of shaved pubes.

"You like *hair*?"

"I like women to look like women, not twelve-year-olds."

"Me, the less hair the better." He goes back to the girl on the screen. "She has *some* hair. You should fuck her." He slides the laptop closer to me. "Read her reviews — all tens."

I need to take my glasses off to read the reviews, but I don't. The words are a blur.

"What do you think?"

"About?"

"Fucking her."

"I'd be nervous."

"That's what Cialis is for. I'll give you a pill. I've got plenty. You'll be able to fuck for hours."

Truthfully, fucking for *hours* sounds exhausting, particularly in my current state.

267

I feel myself being drawn in further, despite my resistance. I tell Evan I don't want to take the pill.

He assures me that Cialis is not addictive, that he uses it all the time, that I will love it, that it will give me a hard-on like I am sixteen. "Take the pill," he says as if I have already agreed to hire the hooker.

I ask a logical question: "How much do they charge?"

"Five hundred, but they expect a tip. More for anything exotic." He raises an eyebrow, then fumbles in his jacket, comes out with a pen and hands it to me. "Write down her number."

I remind him I'm not a member. He tells me I can use his membership.

He waits. When I do nothing he plucks the pen out of my hand, writes the girl's number on a cocktail napkin, and crushes it into my shirt pocket. *"Call her,"* he says. "You'll feel better."

He closes the laptop with a snap, as if he's concluded a successful business transaction.

We drink more wine and talk about other things, none of them memorable. But how could they be, after that?

When we say good night he reminds me to call the call girl.

I leave the restaurant and walk a few

blocks. Though it's December and cold, I need to clear my head. After a while I hail a cab and sag into the backseat.

At home, the emptiness hits me and I realize that despite the absurdity of the evening it was totally distracting, as if I'd gone to see a play, or had performed in one.

As I'm undressing I find the napkin with the girl's number. I don't even look at it. I just throw it away.

34
"That's Cool"

It is a little over a year since Joy has died. I am standing, drink in hand, at an academic cocktail party surrounded by colleagues and students, maybe fifty or sixty people, when a young woman approaches, says hi, and asks if I recognize her.

"You were a student of mine," I say, and take her in: pretty, petite, big dark eyes lined with kohl, bleached platinum hair, nails lacquered black, the distinct scent of smoke and leather about her.

A Proustian moment: the smell of cigarettes and leather, a dude ranch vacation, one of the few family vacations that included my father. On the second day he insisted upon going on the advanced trail ride because his fifteen-year-old son was and if I could do it, surely he could. (I'd been riding in summer camp for several years, but my father, the Queens boy, had never been on a horse.) I'll never forget the sight of him, white knuckles gripping the saddle, fear in his eyes as our horses cantered across an open field, a memorable and vivid image I took pleasure in for many years.

"But you don't remember my name, do you?" she asks, an edginess that borders on belligerence, head cocked to the side.

"No, sorry. I can't recall." I tell her I've had a lot of students over the years, though I remember her well.

"That's cool, it's been ten years," she says and supplies her name, "Ronny, with a *y*, not an *i*."

"Of course, Veronica."

"Ronny," she says, insistent.

Small talk ensues for a few minutes.

Then she says, "I had a terrible crush on you when you were my professor."

I have to smile, and say, "Goes with the territory. But outside of class, you can see I'm just an ordinary guy."

Ronny's dark eyes narrow, assessing me. She tells me about her boyfriend. (Disappointing, as I had momentarily deluded myself with the thought that she was flirting.) They have been together several years. His name sounds familiar and it turns out that he too was a former student, though I can't picture him.

"You're married, right?" she asks.

I hesitate, then tell her that my wife has died a little over a year ago and her cockiness deflates and her sharp face softens and it looks as though she might cry and I steel myself, but she doesn't. She says she's sorry and asks how I'm doing and how my wife died, but I don't answer, and we stand there another moment until she asks if I want to get a drink. I hold up my wineglass indicating that I already have one and she says, "I meant, away from here."

I think, *Why not?*

It is a cool night, but pleasant. We walk about five or six Brooklyn blocks without saying much until we arrive at a bar. Inside, it's noisy, crammed, smoky, loud music blaring. I immediately want out, the noise too much for me, but she leads me to a back room with tables, half-empty and quieter, and we order drinks and food (I am suddenly ravenous), and while I eat a burger she sips red wine and picks at a salad and tells me more about her boyfriend, though I haven't asked ("We haven't slept together in a year and we're breaking up and I think he might be gay though he says he's bi, which is totally cool but . . ."). She keeps talking, switching topics, to her work, what she's writing, "a terrible novel," then asks me what I've read lately and when I tell her not much, she asks, "What's your favorite novel?"

"*Lolita,*" I say, too late feeling as if it is inappropriate or too loaded for the situation, but she's never read it.

She says she thinks writing is defined by gender and how it's harder to be a woman now than it was fifty years ago because women's roles are less defined, but when I ask her if she'd rather be a fifties housewife she makes a face. She tells me that once she breaks up with her boyfriend, she is finished with men, then quickly amends that by saying "men my age, who are immature and self-involved."

She can't possibly be telling me she is interested in a man more than *twice* her age, like me, can she?

She says she is ready to leave Brooklyn, to leave New York. She says she wants to have a quiet life but is afraid she will miss everything, afraid life will pass her by, afraid that everything she ever learned about anything, including writing, is "bogus," then adds as an afterthought, "but not your class, which was great," and I laugh, but she says she's serious. She continues to list more things she is afraid of — that she's not talented enough, not smart enough, that she attracts the wrong men, the wrong friends, that she is afraid of growing old and ending up alone. I tell her it's way too soon for her to worry about that. I feel as if I am her therapist, or worse, her father, and when I say so she gives me a piercing look and tells me that her parents divorced when she was a kid and that she hardly ever sees her father, who is an "asshole," and she does not believe in therapy though she has been seeing a shrink since she was twelve, and I can't help it, I laugh, and she does too, and both of us relax for the first time.

She apologizes for talking too much and asks if I'd like to come back to her place and I laugh again and she says, "What?" I don't know if I should be direct, if I should ask if she is inviting me over to have sex because maybe I'm wrong, because maybe she is inviting me over to continue being her therapist, so I say, "Why?" and she lays her hand over mine and I stifle a tremor and tell her I am too old for her and she asks how old but makes a guess before I can answer, which is fifteen years younger than I am and I (shamelessly) do not correct her, but ask, *What about your boyfriend?* She says he'll be out all night and I pay the bill and we walk through more Brooklyn streets and I feel foolish and awkward (not fifteen years younger than I am, but fifteen years old!). She reaches for my hand and laces her fingers through mine and I stop walking and say, "We can't do this."

"Why not?"

I say something about being her teacher and she reminds me it's been well over a decade and I ask if she's fulfilling some kind of schoolgirl fantasy and she tugs her hand out of mine, angles a look at me, and hisses, *"Schoolgirl?"*

I apologize and we start walking again.

Her apartment is in a brownstone, a fifth-floor walk-up, and I try not to huff as we get to her floor. It's bigger than I imagined, with a large open living room and lots of paintings on the walls ("my boyfriend's, he switched from writing to painting") and stacks of books ("mine, my boyfriend never reads, though he pretends to"). The bedroom is a mess, bed unmade, books everywhere, clothes draped over chairs, looped over doorknobs, sneakers and work boots beside the bed ("my boyfriend's"), all of which add to my discomfort though she seems fine about it. The place reeks of tobacco and leather.

She asks if I want a drink, she has beer and wine in the fridge, "probably some dope somewhere," she says, tugging open a dresser drawer and coming out with a half-smoked joint, which she lights. I move the bf's clothes and perch uneasily on the edge of a chair. I watch her inhale, decline a hit, though I accept a beer, which I chug. I am as nervous as a college boy.

After the weed she asks if it's okay if she smokes a cigarette and I tell her it's fine. Though I haven't smoked in decades I still like the scent. I ask her why the place smells of leather.

"My perfume," she says. "Tuscan Leather. I never wore anything until a year ago when I was at this event and they were giving out free samples. I liked it because it didn't smell like perfume."

I tell her I like it too.

"I think it smells like a man," she says.

"Must be why I like it," I say and we both laugh.

She leans over and kisses me lightly then harder and I kiss her back. She leads me to the messy bed. I stumble over the boyfriend's work boots and for a moment see the absurdity of the situation but it's too late, a part of me already committed to this while the other half watches, raising an eyebrow.

I am just cogent enough and self-conscious enough to ask her to turn off the lights, and she does. (I want to see her but I don't want her to see *me,* or maybe I don't want anyone or anything to be seen.)

After sex, she tells me it was great and not at all like it is with her boyfriend. I don't bother to say the obvious — that if they haven't had sex in over a year how does she remember, that perhaps anything would be better.

She tells me she has always liked older men.

I don't say anything. When I feel enough time has passed, I get up and get dressed.

She asks if she will see me again and I say of course though I don't think so.

On the subway ride back to Manhattan I am gleeful but guilty, as if I have committed a crime.

She texts me later that night: that was nice

I text back: yes

Less than a week passes before she texts me again: drink?

I text back: sure

The fact is, I have been thinking about her. A lot.

I meet her in Brooklyn and it's pretty much a replay of the last time though I am less nervous. Afterward, she tells me that she told her boyfriend about us and he thought it was "cool," and that he always liked me. I have no idea what to say to that.

We maintain this relationship for several months; we talk very little. Actually, that's not true. *I* talk very little. Ronny talks incessantly. About her work, her life, her dreams and aspirations, her parents, her father, whom she hates (Yes, Dr. Freud, I get it), her boyfriend, who has nowhere else to live so he's not moving out, which is cool with her. Throughout our months together I feel relatively detached, as if only a part of me is participating, and you know which part, but I enjoy being with her. Plus, she demands nothing of me. For a while.

After another couple of months she asks if she can meet some of my friends. I don't say yes or no, but there is no way that's happening, particularly as none of my friends even know she exists. She asks if I want to meet her friends. I don't say anything to that either and she pouts for a minute, then shrugs and says, "That's cool." She asks, not for the first time, why we never go to my apartment and when I shake my head and mumble she says that's cool too. Occasionally we go out for drinks or dinner in Brooklyn, though I am always nervous we will meet someone I know. That never happens. Once or twice we meet people she knows who seem perfectly *cool* with meeting me, though I have no idea if they understand the nature of our relationship. She is a nice young woman and I have grown fond of her. I know I keep her in a compartment, apart from the rest of my life, apart from any real feelings. She is a Band-Aid, a soothing balm I take out every once in a while to put over my pain.

I start feeling bad about this around three months in, the same time Ronny tells me she thinks she is falling in love with me, that she hates all the boys her age and it's great being with an older man but that it's okay if I'm not into it because she gets it, with all I've gone through. I tell her it has nothing to do with what I've gone through, but I don't say anything else for a few minutes because I am essentially speechless. All I can think is that she must have been treated badly by a lot of men and that she has, once again, made a bad choice. I finally say something like "You think you love me because I'm nice and paternal," and she gets really pissed and sulks for a few minutes, then paints on a smile and says, "That's cool," though I can see it is not.

I start thinking seriously about how I am going to get out of this. She is a lovely girl, but whatever this is we are having feels inappropriate, which is, I feel, at least in part, what has attracted her to me. There is no other explanation.

I point this out to her and we stop seeing each other for a few weeks, only to start again.

A month or so later we are in her bed when I hear movement in the living room and start to bolt up.

She tells me to chill, that it's just her boyfriend, who, a minute later, knocks, then simultaneously walks in and sits on the edge of the bed, as if he lives here — and he does.

I recognize him right away, tall, skinny, nice-looking though scruffy, with longish disheveled hair, a sad mustache, and terribly bitten fingernails.

He asks how we are doing.

Ronny says, "We're cool."

I think: *Maybe you are.*

He stretches out along the base of the bed, locks his hands behind his head, kicks off his boots, says he's had a terrible day, and starts complaining about someone he works with who is "a douche" and how he's got to get out of there, talking on and on and on.

I am naked under the covers, feeling as if I want to get as far away from here as possible. She is sitting up, bare breasts exposed. But why not, he's her boyfriend, after all, lying at the edge of the bed, *his* bed, complaining about his lousy workday to his girlfriend and the much older man she is sleeping with, who also happens to have been his teacher a dozen years ago.

I would like to vaporize myself.

He says he is sorry to hear about my wife and everything inside me goes rigid. I do not want her mentioned. Not here. I say, "How are you?" It's all I can think to say, the two of them so totally casual and "cool" and me, not at all. He says fine, then talks about some friend who got a show on the Lower East Side and how he is a better painter so it should have been him, and she commiserates. I tell them I've got to go, but I don't move because the only way I can leave is to get up and walk naked to the chair across the room to get to my clothes.

She tells me not to go. The boyfriend says the same thing, then says, "Hey, do you guys mind if I join you?" very casually, already moving toward us. The two of them exchange a look, almost a smile, and I wonder if this has been planned. I say I've got to go and he tells me to chill, and she says the same thing as he eases himself between us, still talking about his bad day while tugging off his skinny jeans, and all I want is to get out of there, an old man in a messy Brooklyn bedroom with two young people who think everything is "cool." It is an absurd cartoon. (Later, I think how I could easily draw a short comic version of the event, but of course I never do.)

There is a bit more to that night (like bolting across the room, tugging on my pants, shoving my underpants into my pocket, stepping into shoes without socks), but enough to say that it was the last time I saw this young woman. There was one long phone call when I told her it was an impossible situation for me, and not good for her, and I think she was crying though she said it was cool. She texted me a few times and I responded, but after a while we both stopped. And that was it. I had to let it go.

There was, for a while, something tender and sweet about this relationship and it was surely a distraction, though I'm really not sure why *she* did it.

Why did I choose this woman, this situation, and not the others? I think because it was so entirely different from what I'd had in the past, because it was improbable, because it could not possibly become anything serious (at least not in my mind).

I told very few people about this, though I did tell my good friends Jane and David, Jane not at all scornful or judgmental of my behavior. In fact, she thought it was good for me, telling me not to dismiss what could turn out to be a good relationship. The other person I told, also a friend, a man in his seventies with three ex-wives, the last one twenty-five years his junior, thought I was a complete jerk, not for having the affair, but for thinking there was anything wrong with it.

35
WHY MEN CAN'T
GRIEVE IN PUBLIC

It is midsummer, almost two years since Joy has died, I am at a dinner party at the upstate home of a retired magazine and book editor, the guests a mix of writers, editors, a few people who have traded in the rat race to become "gentlemen farmers." Everyone appears to know one another. Other than the hostess, Nan, I know no one. There are twelve of us around a long rectangular table. I am at one end, beside Nan.

The table is lit with candles, the food good, the wine flowing. I have already downed two glasses of a full-bodied red.

Midway through dinner, a discussion ensues concerning a grief memoir that, by chance, I have just finished reading, *In a Dark Wood,* by Joseph Luzzi. It is a small book, in no way a bestseller, so I'm surprised when it comes up.

For almost a year I had not been able to read anything; nowadays I read a lot, mostly about death and grieving. I started with Elisabeth Kübler-Ross, the death guru, but she made me feel as if I'd been doing it all wrong, which only added to my grief and my anger (she would say my anger *stage*). According to my interpretation of her writing I had been "cycling" back and forth between shock and grief, something she suggests holds one back from moving toward inevitable "acceptance."

Unlike Kübler-Ross's codified stages, to me the grieving process feels more like a salad, all of the stages tossed together. Unable to control my scrambled emotions, I have often felt as if I were in free fall, as if I'd jumped out of a plane without a parachute.

A writer friend had recommended the Luzzi memoir, a strange though haunting book in which Luzzi, who'd lost his pregnant wife in a car accident (though the baby survived), looks at his grief through the eyes of Dante.

Everyone at the table seems annoyed by the book.

I understand it can feel like an academic book and occasionally cold, the way the author distances us from the tragedy. But I think it's his way of getting closer to understanding it, and it was, to me, extremely interesting. Reading the book I remember thinking, *His tragedy is worse than mine.*

Not that I think there is a hierarchy to loss. Loss is loss. Universal. Nonhierarchical. And yet, one's own loss always feels like the worst loss because no matter how much we empathize with others, we can't quite *feel* their loss or experience it. It's why those one-size-fits-all how-to-get-over-your-loss-and-grief books don't work. Though we can intellectualize another's pain and suffering I'm not sure it's possible to take it in on a personal level. One's own tragedy is always the worst tragedy. I see examples of this on a daily basis. People say, "I know how you feel because . . ." and immediately launch into their own story of loss — aunt, uncle, father, mother, dog, cat.

It turns out that several of the guests know Luzzi, or knew his late wife, and the dialogue has become heated, fueled by resentment, the general consensus: *How dare he write this book about his dead wife, having remarried and produced a child with wife number two!* (It is, I should add, ten years since Luzzi's first wife has died.)

The hostess, Nan, a warm, intelligent woman, a widow of many years, who knows my situation, is talking to me quietly apart from the group about an organization we

both belong to and I realize that she is trying to shield me from the general conversation, but I do not want to be protected.

"Why write it *now*?" a woman at the far
end of the table barks.

"He must need the money," says another.

As I am already writing my own book, this
discussion brings up a question I have been
grappling with: If the survivor writes a book
about the death of his or her partner, is it in
some way exploitative? A question I have
asked myself many times, and a tough one
to answer — the idea of making my loss
public and possibly profiting from it is dis-
turbing.

"Maybe he needed the time to come to
terms with the death of his wife," I say.

"Ten *years*?" says the first woman, leaning forward as if ready to lunge at me.

"I don't think there's a shelf life on grieving," I say.

"He's remarried," she says, as if this is
some sort of proof of his betrayal, "and
they've had a *child*." Then she pauses and
adds more quietly, "I knew his first wife."

I get it. Why she is condemning him.
Because it appears he's gotten over the
death of his first wife, her friend. I stop hat-
ing her. I want to explain it: that you do not
get *over* the loss; that just because you've

started a new life and formed a new relationship, it does not negate your feelings of loss; that it is entirely possible to air those feelings years later, even more possible that Luzzi has been grappling with his book and how to find a way to express his grief for all of those ten years, despite having a new wife and child.

What I say is, "I think for anyone who writes a book like this, it's cathartic, no matter *when* you write it. And for a writer it's more than that, it simply makes sense — a way to put your feelings on the page and look at them, something artists do all the time."

"But he's not an artist," the woman says, and the man beside her, her husband or partner, nods his head in agreement.

"He's a Dante scholar," I say, "someone who is used to writing about his ideas. And this is his second book."

The woman admits she has never read Luzzi's books. I want to ask how she can possibly criticize a book she has not read, but it turns out that *no one* at the dinner party — all of whom have been chiming in with their criticism — has read the book.

I cannot help myself. It's time to offer up my "credentials" in the game of loss. I tell them I've not only read Luzzi's book but that I lost my wife, quite suddenly, a little less than two years ago.

The table goes quiet.

I did not mean to exploit my loss to show that I know what I'm talking about or to prove that I am right.

Or did I?

Now the group wants to hear what I have to say, all of them leaning forward, waiting.

I take a sip of wine. I apologize for bringing the dinner party down, but the guests urge me on.

As I explain that I am writing about my wife's sudden death it produces in me a mix of complex feelings. Am I, in some twisted way, playing the martyr, or is this genuinely who I have become, not only a widower, but a spokesperson for grieving men who are not allowed to openly grieve, yet condemned if they do not grieve enough?

I point out that as a grieving man I am constantly told to *stop* grieving, to get on with my life, to get laid, to find happiness, to remarry. I add that women are not only *allowed* to grieve openly, but are *supposed to,* though I've heard people criticize women who marry too soon after their husbands die, so maybe this cuts both ways.

"You know, get on with your life and be

happy," I say, "but not *too* soon and not *too* happy."

This produces a few nervous giggles, but no one disputes me. I am the expert.

Of course I am not. I just want my dinner companions to see that writing about loss is complicated and risky, that it opens you up to the criticism of others, which they cannot dispute as they are doing just that.

I bring up another book I've just read, *Widow,* by Lynn Caine, written in 1974 (possibly one of the first books of its kind and apparently a bestseller), given to me by a friend (a widow). In the way my dinner companions were irritated by the Luzzi book, I had a similar reaction to Caine's book, though I was annoyed for different reasons. It's a very basic book (Caine, a book publicist at the time, immediately states she is not a writer, though her book makes the point that anyone can write about loss, and I think that's fair to say).

I explain to the group how the first half of Caine's book is honest and good, the author's emotions real, raw and angry. But that the second half, with its unrelenting emphasis on widowhood and the plight of the widow to the total exclusion of men or even a nod to the *idea* that men can have such feelings — or *any* feelings — was, to me, infuriating.

"I get that it might be harder for women, particularly in 1974, and that it's obvious Caine was writing for women and widows, but she makes it seem as if men not only have no feelings about loss, but they all go blithely forward, quickly replacing the dead wife with a new one."

"A lot of men *do* remarry quickly," says the woman at the other end of the table, though she is softer now, no longer on the attack.

"So do some women," I say, "but men, women, even if they remarry, it doesn't mean they've gotten over their loss."

Now the group is talking about gender stereotypes, and I add how the culture encourages men to move on while secretly condemning them for it.

"You know," I say. "To the newly married widower's face, *Good for you!* Behind his back, *Do you believe he remarried in less than a year!*"

I get a few more laughs.

I'd like to add more, but I've pretty much said it: that loss remains a part of you, a hole or a void that you will carry forever, no matter how you try to fill it, no matter how much happiness you bring into your life, whether you remarry or not, and I don't think remarrying (or not) is a bad or good thing, and that's true for all genders.

Instead, I talk about Caine's insistence that women get their "identity" from their husbands, which generates a healthy back-and-forth about men and women, husbands and wives.

I sit back while the group talks and argues and think how Joy very much had her own identity apart from mine, an identity she fought for, and how we *reflected* each other but did not identify ourselves through each other.

For me, that meant I lost a partner in the true sense of that word: someone who reflected *me* back to *me* (which sounds like the ultimate narcissism, but Joy reflected both the good me and the bad me). We shared our work and our life. Joy was not just a "wife," with its outdated definitions and implications of a person who takes care of the home, cooks, cleans, and raises the kids. (Though the bulk of child rearing often does fall on the mother, and did on Joy, my daughter spent much of her infant days in my studio while Joy worked in an office.)

Nan says she hopes we've come a long way from 1974 and those rigid gender identities.

I agree, but add that I still think there are

certain things men can get away with that women cannot, and vice versa. "And from what I've observed and experienced in my current status, I'd say the culture expects men and women to behave in certain prescribed ways."

But I am starting to feel weary. It is not easy being a spokesperson. The only thing I want to say, to affirm, is that men suffer loss as much as women. It's just that they're not supposed to show it — although they'll be condemned if they do not.

On my way home I wonder what Joy would have thought — if I was showing off; if I needed to win?

The only thing I know for sure is that we would have discussed it.

36
"MR. LONELY"

A hot day, the sky over Manhattan the off-white color of old newsprint, the city's never-ending noise working my nerves, a million thoughts coming and going like gnats nipping at my brain. I am in the throes of so many decisions, big and small — the biggest, whether or not I should sell my loft — and I can't figure out what to do. I have discussed, deliberated, and dissected the idea with friends, who I suspect are sick of hearing from me, sick of my waffling, sick of my inability to make a decision. If Joy were here she would be equally sick of my equivocating, but she would *tell* me what to do. It's funny, because in the past when she told me what to do, I didn't like it, but time and absence have a way of idealizing the things we did not like or appreciate.

I remember helping my mother clean out my father's closets after he died, listening to her idealize him until I'd finally had enough.

"In case you forgot," I said, in a teasing tone, "he was also a pain in the ass." My mother didn't miss a beat: "But he was *my* pain in the ass."

I have pretty much forgotten the fights Joy and I had, the moments of exasperation, the times our friend Jane Kent calls "molecule moments," when you hate every molecule in your partner's body, and there were plenty. It became a joke between us, something to say in the middle of an argument, "I'm having a molecule moment," which could often defuse it (though not always).

Today, I'd give anything for a molecule moment. I've had enough of this dead-is-forever shit. I want Joy back. I need her quiet counsel, even if it comes with a side order of irritation.

I try reading for a class, working on a short story, editing student pages, but nothing soothes my restless mind.

I decide to draw. It will calm me. But *what*?

I sit at my drawing table for ten minutes but my brain will not stop whirring.

I put my pencils down and head out, south on Seventh Avenue toward Whole Foods, an invented destination — I could use a few things in my fridge (orange juice, yogurt, a bagel) so it will appear as if someone lives in my loft, however slight the evidence.

As I walk, I try to formulate answers to the myriad questions I have been asking Joy in my head but as usual, she does not answer.

People pass by, everyone in a rush except for tourists lingering over maps or staring up at buildings, blocking the sidewalk. Though I am not in a hurry, I want to scream at them — *MOVE!*

I am the rudest, ugliest New Yorker, in a race to get nowhere.

A young couple dares to stop me with a gentle question concerning directions. Have they missed the scowl on my face? They are French, in their twenties, adorable and lost. I manage not to bark at them, to speak to them in my terrible French and not only give them directions, but make suggestions as to where they should eat. They tell me that my French is good (a lie) and thank me profusely. I watch them head off hand in hand and feel sad.

Less than a minute later an elderly couple passes, also holding hands, the way I imagined Joy and I would when we grew old. They see me staring and smile. I try to smile back though I'm not sure my facial muscles are working correctly; it feels more like a twitch.

Another couple is just behind them, tall and very good-looking, perfectly torn jeans and T-shirts with enigmatic sayings, their arms wound around each other's waist.

I hate them.

It's as if someone cruel is choreographing this walk among the coupled.

I duck into Whole Foods, but the place is a cornucopia of more attractive couples, as if someone from Central Casting has stocked the place with the best, the brightest, and only the coupled — and me shopping for one.

Poor me.

And with that thought the pity party I have been throwing for myself splinters and shatters and I have a kind of out-of-body experience where I watch myself move up and down the Whole Foods aisles accompanied by a sound track of Paul Anka's "Lonely Boy," and it suddenly seems hilarious. Soon it becomes a game, a challenge: how many "lonely" songs can I play in my head while shopping? "Only the Lonely," "Are You Lonesome Tonight?," "All By Myself," "Eleanor Rigby," "Mr. Lonely" (the old Bobby Vinton version and rap star Akon's newer, chipmunk-inspired rendition). It is a stand-up comic's routine about his lonely-guy life.

I buy bagels, muffins, cookies, mac and cheese from the hot tray, comfort food, and I deserve comfort, don't I? A chorus of "Mr. Lonely" plays in my mind and I snort a laugh. I know Joy would head for the produce aisle, so I make a side trip to get an avocado, my idea of a vegetable. I imagine Joy looking at my cart with disapproval, so I add a few apples.

On the checkout line another beautiful couple, this one with an adorable four- or five-year-old, pulls up alongside me. For a moment, I am intensely jealous of what appears to be their perfect life. I note the mostly fresh food in their cart and the fact that their toddler is scarfing down an eight-dollar artisanal chocolate bar.

But the couple is arguing.

She says, "Did you have to give him *that,* you *always* . . ." and he says, "I did it to keep him quiet, must you make a big deal about *everything* . . ."

I am no longer jealous. I'm glad not to be fighting. But a nanosecond later I am jealous of that too, the interaction, the back-and-forth, even the sarcasm. I want to say, *Don't fight, guys, it could all end tomorrow,* but of course I don't. I turn to the kid and say, "Yum, that looks good," and the little tyke stretches his chocolate-covered hand out, offering me a bite or a lick, which I turn down but thank him and tell him he is a very nice and generous boy, and the parents smile at their child with pride, then at me, and then at one another. I smile back. I am starting to get the hang of this human interaction thing, not wanting to kill people for no reason, not envying them for an appearance of perfection, remembering that nothing is perfect, but good enough.

When I get back to the loft, I eat one of the apples. It makes me feel healthy and altruistic. I hold it up and say, "See?" as if letting Joy know.

I spend some time doing schoolwork, then get my pad and pencils. I know exactly what I want to draw: me.

I made this drawing staring into a mirror. I needed to see what I looked like *now,* what other people see when they look at me. After the initial shock of really studying myself — noticing how my upper eyelids have become heavy, how the lines around my mouth have deepened, how my face has become fuller — I was able to detach and like with any other drawing took in the overall shape, breaking the parts of my face into sections, then features, projections, recessions, every-

thing reduced to the usual line, tone, and mark. My daughter says I always make people look better in my drawings, but I think I was a bit harsh with myself or else this really is what I look like now — not much like the young man who got married more than forty years ago and different from the way I looked when Joy died almost three years ago.

I look at the finished sketch. It feels incomplete, but I know what I want to add.

I saw Joy beside me, and sketched her in using a harder pencil to create a more delicate drawing. I consider going further,

drawing Joy more completely and definitively because she was never in the background as she appears here, but I like the somewhat ethereal quality and the way it captures the evanescence of her smile, and the youthful quality Joy always possessed. I like that she is a smiling presence to my severe one. I like that there is no existing photograph like this. I could have found one — there are dozens and dozens of photos of the two of us together — but it's not what I wanted. I wanted a composite: each of us separate but brought together, as we were in life, each our own person, but a unit.

37
CODA TO A MEDICAL MYSTERY

I lost the emergency room doctor's card, then found his name scribbled on a piece of paper a week or so later, though no one at the hospital knew who he was, or if they did, they weren't telling me.

That was only the beginning.

The city coroner's office had no record of an autopsy either.

Months passed. I couldn't take it anymore. I wanted answers. A part of me believed, or wanted to believe, that knowing exactly how my wife had died would help me deal with it.

Thwarted by the hospital, I finally consult a group of lawyers.

They need to see our will, which I turn over, but for some reason it has been un-stapled (I knew not why, or when), but now the unstapled document has to be validated by the lawyer who had drawn it up or the courts will not accept it. Not so easy. The lawyer has retired and it will take more than a Google search and several months to locate him. Finally he is found, and the will approved. Back it goes to the surrogate court, where it sits for several more months. Eventually the court approves it and I am, finally and officially, the executor of my wife's estate — all of which takes well over a year from the time of Joy's death.

Now my lawyers can petition the hospital for the autopsy. They write letters. They call. No response. They write more letters and make more calls. Nothing. Is this gross inefficiency? Or something more? The lawyers are getting irritated; so am I. They suggest I go to the hospital to try to get the autopsy results in person, and so, reluctantly, I go. At the hospital's Records Office I explain that my lawyers have been writing and calling. The woman in the Records Office claims they have no record of anyone ever inquiring. I stifle a scream and fill out new forms. She assures me the autopsy results will be sent to me. I wait. Weeks pass. Nothing arrives.

I consult my lawyers. They urge me to go back to the hospital.

Is it even necessary to say that going into that place, walking through those corridors and standing in the hallways where I sat and stood and paced for hours waiting to hear if my wife would live or die, brings everything back in graphic detail? I relive the day with each visit, now accompanied by aggravation and frustration. On the third visit I am told there is no autopsy, that one has never been performed. *How can this be?* The hospital has no answer. But if no autopsy has been performed, when I am certain one has been (I had approved it with the emergency room doctor, still unknown to *anyone,* which only contributes to the idea that I have imagined him), it means I will never learn how my wife has actually died, because it is too late to perform another. I picture the dour undertaker eyeing the box of ashes when I asked him if the autopsy had been performed.

I leave the hospital and walk crosstown, angry, frustrated, and incredulous. I've gone only a few blocks when I start to get a migraine, full-blown by the time I get home. I take my meds, lie in bed with a dark cloth over my eyes, and watch the electric eel do its dance. I *know* I signed forms for an autopsy. I call my sister-in-law and we discuss how this could possibly have happened. I call my daughter. "I *think* you authorized an autopsy," she says, "at least you told me you did." (Not exactly proof, but I am certain I have.)

So what is going on?

I call the lawyers again. They tell me to go back to the hospital and demand my wife's medical records, which I do, the next day.

There is a different woman at the Records Office. After getting more runaround — *Oh, the records should have been sent to you by now* — *maybe the autopsy was never performed* — *maybe it was, but got lost* — it is my turn to lose it.

I storm out of the Records Office and through the hospital, furious and determined to find a hospital administrator, and I do.

I tell her my story (rant is more like it), and add, "If this isn't fixed, if this autopsy is lost, or worse, was never performed, I am suing this fucking hospital!"

I have no idea if I can sue or not, but I am, at that moment, out of my mind with fury, and it seems like the right kind of threat.

In fact, the hospital administrator is a very nice woman, middle-aged and solid-looking in her navy blue suit, a kind face and soft voice. She calms me down. She walks me back to the Records Department. She uses her clout, which is impressive — everyone is suddenly courteous and helpful. Within minutes — *minutes* — the autopsy results are located! Amazing, *But how?* Or, more important, had they ever been lost?

The woman in the Records Department says they will have the newly found autopsy results faxed over from another department. Minutes later, the fax machine whirs and starts printing, then stops dead after two pages. They try again. Same thing. As this is all happening at the end of the workday the Records Department woman suggests I come back in the morning and she will have it ready for me then. *No way!* I don't believe her. The hospital administrator steps in again. Together, we get everyone's name, along with the number of the newly found autopsy file. For some reason they are not allowed to give me the two printed pages, only the entire report, which apparently runs to twenty-plus pages. This, after saying, for close to two years, that it did not even exist.

The hospital administrator assures me it is all a mistake, and that the autopsy report will be ready for me in the morning. One more time I walk crosstown. I feel semisuccessful though worried. Will there be another last-minute glitch or obstruction? Will someone "lose" the autopsy again?

Halfway home, another thought slithers

into my mind: *What will the autopsy show?*

The words of the mysterious emergency room doctor play in my mind: "We may never know."

I do not sleep much that night.

The next morning I head back to the hospital still anxious that something or someone will have intervened and I will not get the report. But I am wrong. The report is ready and waiting, sealed in a large manila envelope.

I tell myself not to read it, that it will undoubtedly upset me, then find a quiet corridor in the hospital, sit on a bench, open the envelope, and begin to read. It is extensive, and not all of the medical jargon makes sense, though enough does, enough to see there is no cause of death. *How can that be?* I scan the twenty-odd pages over and over. Everywhere the question is posed — *Cause of Death* — the same word is typed — *none* — or it is left blank.

No embolism. No heart attack. Not even conjecture.

We may never know.

I call the lawyers. They say to messenger the report right over.

The next day, one of the lawyers calls to say that she and her colleagues are as baffled as I am by the fact that there is no stated cause of death. She asks if they might send it out to a few doctors to read, and of course I say yes.

It is a few days before the lawyer gets back to me.

She explains that two doctors have read the autopsy results and agree — no embolism, no heart attack. Also, that the doctors suggested the autopsy report go to a pharmacologist, and so it has already been sent to two, both of whom have agreed on a cause of death.

She pauses. I wait.

"It appears . . ." she says. I hear her take a breath. "That your wife had been prescribed drugs that interacted in her system and" — another intake of breath — "that's what killed her."

Images come back to me in a rush — Joy's flushed face and fever, the fact that she felt unwell and how it had progressed so quickly over the course of the day.

For a moment I say nothing. I had been resigned to the fact of an embolism or a heart attack, something practically unpreventable once it starts, and there was some consolation in that — that no way I could have saved her.

I tell the lawyer I need a minute, that I will call her back.

I pace the length of my loft then go out. I can't stay in, can't sit still. I take a long walk through the city streets with no destination. It is as if I have to rethink everything about Joy's death, and I don't want to. I've been through enough grief, have come to a point of near-acceptance, but this presents a whole new scenario that means understanding her death as something that should never have happened, that *could* have been prevented.

The next day the lawyers suggest I take legal action. Once again, I tell them I need time to think it over.

I call my daughter. She is outraged. At *me.* How can I even hesitate? "If it had been *you,* Mom would have already started the lawsuit — and she'd have *won!*"

I know there is some truth in this. But the idea of having to relive Joy's death in depositions and court, now, two years later, is not something I want to do.

Another day and sleepless night pass before I reluctantly agree to go forward.

This discovery has added another layer of darkness over what happened. My nightmares, which were starting to ease, have recurred, now coupled with visions of men in white, whispering and conspiring.

Why else was the autopsy "missing" —

"lost" — "never performed"? Could that all be a coincidence? Was the hospital just lax, hopelessly disorganized, or helping to cover up a mistake that had resulted in death?

I don't know and I can't say.

I try my best to ignore it as I am told the case could go on for years. But there is no way to ignore it when the lawyers ask me to figure out my wife's worth in dollar value — what her future books could have earned, or her lost teaching salary, or her speaking fees, and more.

What saves me as I write down these figures is hearing Joy's voice in my head, "Don't forget I was already in discussion about a documentary, and I was planning a sequel to *Food City,* and a novel based on a woman in the early brewery industry" — all the things she had planned and talked about doing come back as I write, what she believed she would accomplish, so many of the projects already sketched out or even begun.

So what is a human life worth?

It appears it comes down to dollars and cents where the law is concerned.

Suppose my wife were an "ordinary" woman. By that I mean one who was not writing books or teaching, but a housewife, without a paying job.

What would she be worth then? Would it be the amount of money the survivor now had to pay a housekeeper or a cook?

Suppose the deceased hadn't worked for years? Would that mean his or her life was worth nothing in dollar value?

These are appalling questions.

I've never seen a less appealing example of our capitalist culture — and I'm a capitalist! I believe in working to make money. In free enterprise. But to figure out what someone — *my wife* — is worth, based entirely on her earning power, sickened me. Is that the only way we have to value a life? It is a distressing and depressing notion.

Of course it makes me think about *my* worth. I teach. I write books, some that have actually made money; I make paintings to show and commissioned paintings for a decent price. But like my wife, everything I do is freelance. I wonder if the law would be more amenable to a husband's freelance work than a wife's?

I wait to hear what the courts will decide. If there is any compensation it will be a dubious reward.

I am reminded of a phone call I received a day or two after that gallery fire. It was from an insurance adjuster, who went over the list of my paintings lost in the blaze, what the gallery said they were worth, and which I had to validate. It was a substantial amount of money. He didn't say anything until the end of the conversation, though here and there he uttered just-audible snorts that indicated annoyance or disbelief. When we finished the accounting he said, "I'll bet you're glad."

"What?" I said. I wasn't sure I'd heard him correctly.

"I know you artists," he said, a sneer in his voice. "You must be happy to be getting all that money for your paintings."

I took a moment, then managed to spit out something like "You have no idea how many years of work those paintings represent, almost all of them sold and borrowed back for the show, and so they were paid for a long time ago — I will receive nothing for them! Whatever insurance money there is will go to those collectors whose paintings were destroyed."

He was quiet a moment, then offered up one monosyllable, "Oh."

He did not say he was sorry.

The next day, having seethed all night, I called the insurance company and located his superior. I repeated what the adjuster had said to me. His boss seemed appropriately outraged on my behalf; he even asked if I wanted the man fired. I said no, I just wanted the company to know what he'd said.

A day or two later the adjuster called back. He apologized, though it sounded half-hearted. I told him that I accepted his apology but I wanted him to think about something: that when someone suffers a loss, no matter what it is, no matter what sort of money is attached to it, he should think before he speaks, before he makes a judgment about what that person is going to gain from the loss, because he has no idea what that is, and if he continued in the insurance business (I think I said insurance *racket*), he might consider developing some empathy. He mumbled another halfhearted apology that sounded more like forced humble pie. Afterward, I wondered if what I'd said had made any impact on him at all.

It gets me thinking about an apology from the surgeon who performed my wife's operation. An apology from a doctor when his patient dies seems appropriate, doesn't it? And there was a time, right after it happened, when it was clear the doctor must have learned that his patient had died (she'd missed her follow-up appointments, and the hospital had to have delivered the news), when a phone call would have gone a long way, something to show me that he cared. But there was nothing. Had his insurance company told him not to call? Had he even considered it?

I don't know the answers.

But there it is, an autopsy report that took almost two years to be found, one that neglected to declare any cause of death — a medical mystery I had no idea existed.

Now I wait to hear if, when, and how it will be resolved.

38
FATHER AND DAUGHTER

It is almost three years after Joy's death that Dorie and I finally say the things we have needed to say, or at least begin to.

Dorie has been living in Los Angeles part-time and has sublet her New York apartment. It means that when she comes to New York — which she does often for work — she lives with me, an arrangement I like.

Less than a week before Dorie arrives for one of these New York trips, I have received terrible news. A very good friend has died. A friend whom Dorie has known since birth. A friend of mine (and Joy's) whom Dorie loves and was able to talk to, a friend who, like Joy, was athletic and health-conscious, who hiked and swam every day, and who, again like Joy, died suddenly and unexpectedly. When her husband — also my good friend — called with the news, my legs buckled, a cartoonish reaction I never believed real or possible.

The news was stunning and for days I was haunted by my friend's death, constantly thinking about her, and the unreality of the loss. Even now, death is impossible to grasp, to believe.

When Dorie arrives I cannot tell her. I do not want to see her tears or witness her pain. Again, I am protecting her. Or am I protecting myself?

Each day I have a new excuse: the day she arrives is too soon, the next day I'm too busy, until I finally run out of excuses.

The fourth day is my birthday, and Dorie and I are planning to go out to dinner. She, like her mother, believes in celebrating birthdays, which I protest, though enjoy when forced.

It is a couple of hours before we are going out when Dorie comes home from a photo shoot. She's tired, she says, and in need of a shower. I stop her. I ask her to sit down. I say, "I have something to tell you."

Her face freezes.

"It's not anything about me," I add quickly. "I'm fine."

"Okay," she says, but I can see she is holding her breath.

I tell her what happened and her face collapses and her eyes fill with tears but I keep up my steady stream of talk — how I needed a few days to process it before I could tell her, how her husband seems okay, how I am okay, and Dorie, stunned and crying now, simply says, "No," and I am hurled back in time to the hospital, to when we got the news from the emergency room doctor, but still, I keep talking, as if talk can somehow make it better or erase it, until, finally, Dorie gets up, says she's taking a shower, and quietly heads down the hall.

A half hour later, she is back, her hair wet, eyes puffy.

"I sobbed in the shower so I wouldn't upset you," she says. It is not an indictment; it is said with kindness and consideration. She is trying to protect my feelings (the ones I don't show), and I realize without saying that I should be consoling her rather than banishing her to the shower where she can sob without upsetting *me*.

I ask her if she still wants to go to dinner, and she says yes.

The restaurant is downtown chic, elegant and understated. We are seated in an expansive back room, quiet except for a table of businesspeople who are drinking, and noisy.

We order wine. For a while we chat about nothing important.

Then Dorie starts talking about our friend

who has died. "She was the one person I could talk to about Mom dying," she says, and for once I do not shut her down. The conversation shifts to Joy's death and soon Dorie is talking about their relationship, the frustration she sometimes had with Joy's quiet reaction to things, and she says, through her tears, that she feels and fears she never knew whole parts of her mother.

It is the first time Dorie has opened up to me like this, and the first time I have ever heard some of the things she is saying. I listen. I let her know that there were times I had the same reaction, though I had years of practice and came to accept Joy's quiet as *thoughtful*.

When Dorie says she is afraid she never got to know her mother and now she never will, I realize that this is *her* burden, the guilt *she* is carrying, so different from my own. I realize something else that I have known but had not truly taken in, that Dorie's loss is not like mine. She lost a mother. I lost a wife. And those are two very different losses.

I tell her that she *did* know her mother, that Joy's quietness was a big part of who she was and how she processed things, that that was something I had to learn, something I now see and hear was not easy for a teenager, or even a young woman. I see how Joy's death has exacerbated Dorie's feeling of things left unsaid and unresolved, and I try to assuage these fears and perhaps I am partially successful, but what is important is that it's the first time I have allowed my daughter to express her feelings, her regrets and her fears in regard to the loss of her mother, and this talk, this opening up between us, brought on by the sudden death of a friend, has been a catalyst that has created an opportunity for intimacy that we have not had, that I have not *allowed* since Joy died.

It is, one might think, a depressing meal, Dorie crying, me welling up, even permitting myself a few real tears, but it is not. The table of drunk businesspeople have left and we are the only two people in the small back room, eating and drinking, sometimes crying, sometimes laughing, and in some ways this is one of our best dinners together.

It is a sad and painful irony that it took another tragedy to help us deal with our own, but there is another realization — that despite the pain, the talk was nothing to be scared of, nothing to run away from, no reason for me to shut it down — that stopping the conversation, as I had in the past, had been harder work, holding my emotions in check, getting my mask in place.

I wonder if I had continued to shut Dorie down, would we have grown apart?

I don't think so, don't think that's possible, not for a father and daughter who mean so much to each other. But we would have missed something.

I realize something else: that I have been writing much of this book for my daughter because it has been too painful for me to *tell* her what happened or how I felt.

Now that the window has been opened, it has allowed us to talk more freely, allowed me to ask: "Why were you so mad at me in Mexico City?"

"Oh, *that,*" says Dorie. "It wasn't about Mom, it was about you needing to leave — and I didn't want to."

"Really?" I say, realizing that I have assigned every bad mood of Dorie's to this lack of communication, when it was not the case. For three years I've been projecting, blaming myself.

"That, and missing the Uber," Dorie says.

"You're not a patient girl," I say with a smile.

"No," she says, "not my strong suit," and laughs.

And it's then, looking at my daughter, who is laughing despite the tears on her cheeks, that I realize we are going to get through this, and that we are going to be just fine.

The next morning I awake in a dream where Joy and Dorie are laughing. I have no idea about what, as if I have arrived too late for the joke, but no matter, it's rare that I have a good dream and I want to extend it, preserve it. I skip breakfast, splash water on my face, and head into my studio propelled by a sense of urgency, the image still resonating on the back of my eyelids, but for how long? I draw rapidly, trying to get it down on paper before it disappears. I have not drawn like this in a long time, as though my pencil is tracing the image in my mind,

yet it feels natural. When the picture starts to fragment and disintegrate I panic — *No, don't go!* — then realize it's okay because I have made a clear sketch of it on the page. Now I go about filling in, completing it.

I take in the drawing and think how much Joy and Dorie look alike, something I never quite saw in real life though other people remarked on it often. I decide I must send this to Dorie so she can see how much physicality she shares with her mother. Perhaps, in some way, it will help her feel that their physical bond extends to a psychic one, and that things left unspoken do not always have to be expressed.

39
LILY II

One day Lily sneezes.

Three days later, she is still sneezing. I bring her to the vet.

The vet confirms it's a cold, nothing serious, though she takes tests that show a half-pound weight loss, not good in an already thin elderly cat, but nothing to be alarmed about either.

Relieved, I take Lily home.

A week later she stops eating. I immediately bring her back to the vet.

The vet weighs her again. Lily has lost over a pound in the week since we've last been here.

The veterinarian, a pretty young woman with an amiable disposition, frowns.

She takes more of Lily's blood. She feels Lily's frail body. I talk to Lily the whole time; "You'll be okay," I say. "Everything will be fine." How is it that I can still put faith in those phrases, that I still believe them? I run my hand along Lily's back, feel her spine too clearly through her fur, which has grown thin. The vet has her hands on Lily's belly, gently probing. She says she would like to do "a few more tests." She and her assistant carry Lily out of the room.

I wait in the small examining room. It is warm but I feel cold. I stare at the white walls, the examining table, the shiny floor.

I squeeze my eyes shut as images from the day Joy died flash in my mind. I take deep breaths. I reread texts and e-mails on my cell phone. I check the clock on the wall again and again.

I close my eyes again and see Lily waiting by the elevator in my loft, howling, under the bed at Yaddo, on my lap, on Joy's lap.

Time is creeping. There is nothing here to distract me.

Finally the vet comes back and gently places Lily onto the examining table. Lily is trembling and I put my arm around her.

I recognize the look on the vet's face before she says, "We took a sonogram and discovered a mass, a *large* mass."

Her diagnosis: an advanced cancer.

I ask what can be done.

"Possibly radiation or chemotherapy, maybe surgery, though I wouldn't recommend it." She pauses. "I think you should euthanize her."

"*What?* When?"

The vet pauses again, then says, "Now."

"But she's still coming into bed at night to be pet, to sleep on my chest or in my arms, and she's always purring."

The vet lays her open palm on Lily's side. "She's purring now," she says. "What a sweetie."

"But she seems okay," I say, almost pleading.

"She will not be okay very soon," the vet says, "but if you want to prolong her life we can get her started on chemo because I don't think she would survive surgery at her age."

I swallow hard. I fight back tears. "I do not want her to suffer," I say. "She's almost nineteen and has had a good life."

The vet tells me I am making the right decision and for a moment I am back in that hospital corridor with the emergency room doctor who is asking me if I will approve an autopsy and I am saying yes and he is nodding approval.

I am not ready to lose Lily, not so fast, not in minutes. But I know the vet is right.

She tells me to take some time with Lily, that she will be back in a while, then she and her assistant slip out.

I crouch down and put my arms fully around Lily's frail little body and she curls against me. I burrow into her fur. I kiss her head and scratch her chin and tell her what a good cat she's been to both Joy and me, and she continues to purr the whole time. We stay like that for ten minutes. I thank her for taking care of me. I cry. Lily purrs. I think of Joy, and how we had not gotten a chance to say good-bye, not even ten minutes.

When the vet and her assistant come back they sedate Lily, her purring turns to a light snore, her furry chin comes to rest on my hand, then the lethal injection and she is gone.

I cry. A lot. Tears streaming down my cheeks.

"I'll bet you see plenty of grown men crying," I say to the vet, sniffing back tears, trying to be funny.

She nods and pats my shoulder, which makes me cry harder. I feel completely undone.

She asks what I want to do with Lily's body and as I sign papers to have her cremated I am back in the funeral home, writing a check and holding the box of ashes.

I leave the vet's office and head down the

street not quite connected, as if I am floating, but it's not a good feeling. What I want to do is to call Joy; I need to tell her about Lily. I call her sister instead. I slump onto the steps of a brownstone and talk to Kathy for several minutes. Afterward, I walk the four blocks home carrying the empty cat carrier. When I get there I clear away Lily's litter box and food bowls, crying the whole time; I cannot stop.

So why could I cry so easily for my cat, but not my wife?

It is several days before I ask myself that question again and come up with a partial answer — that the suddenness of Joy's death, the shock and trauma of it, froze something in me so that I could not cry.

But then I'm not so sure. After all, Lily's death was fast and sudden too.

I think it's something else: that saying good-bye to a pet is simple and direct, the relationship so much less complicated than saying good-bye to a person, to a loved one, and so the tears are easier too; and in some way we are prepared for the death of our pets, their shorter life span a fact we have known from the beginning.

Going into a marriage we don't think about our partner's life span or his or her eventual death despite "till death do us part."

Lily's love had been hard to win, but once I won it she was devoted in the way only a pet can be, unconditionally, trusting and utterly dependent. Maybe we want this in a partner — or think we do — though I suspect an utterly dependent partner, one who loved without any conditions, would eventually grate on the nerves, or they would on mine, though it makes it obvious why people love their pets the way they do.

For months I'd see Lily everywhere. I expected her to be there when I came home, to jump on the bed at night, and I missed her.

Her sudden absence was sad and real but it did not knock me out of my life or crush me in the way that Joy's sudden death had for so long.

Still, it was the right thing to let Lily go. It was her time. And I know Joy would have agreed.

40
FOOD CITY

I am holding a hard copy of *Food City.*

Almost three years after Joy's death, three years of worrying whether or not it would be finished, her epic book is about to be published, to enter the world without her, a glorious if bittersweet legacy — I have to remind myself of that — a big, brilliant story of a largely forgotten history when New York City fed the world, as only Joy could tell it.

I remember the day she decided the story had to be written.

She'd come home from the library to tell me about a discovery, nothing big, she said, but "transformative." She had been researching the book for some time but this was a turning point. She talked about it for a while and afterward I suggested that she write it down, and she did.

A transformative moment (for me) came in the Rare Book Room at the New York Public Library. There, as I leafed through the crumbling pages of the account book of a local nineteenth century merchant I came across a delicate though perfectly pressed bunch of flowers. Was I the first person to look at this ledger since it had been stored in an attic or storeroom over a hundred years ago? Finding the flowers made clear that the manufacturers and their workers, whom I was studying, were real human beings, not just names in a directory or newspaper article.

This was the beginning of a long journey for Joy, who had never really been a writer, and a lot harder one than she imagined. There were moments when she was close to quitting, though she never did.

I remember the night I stood in Joy's office just weeks after her death and vowed I would get her book published. If I'd known then how difficult it was going to be I'd never have made that vow. Thank God I didn't know. In some ways I think it was the same for Joy; if she'd known all the hours, weeks, months that became years of research and writing and rewriting, would

she have signed on for the job so enthusias-
tically?

There is an analogy here to grief: if we knew how much pain there would be, how long it would take for the wound to heal, how many missteps we'd make, how many sleepless nights, how many times we'd think *I just can't do this, I just won't make it,* we probably wouldn't, and yet we do.

I replay the many conversations Joy and I had about her book, the talks, which some-times became fights, and how, at times, I longed for those fights after her death while I worked toward the completion and publi-cation of her book.

My cell phone vibrates. A text from Do-rie, reacting to the photo of *Food City* I sent her just a few moments ago.

OMG. It's gorgeous. Mom would be
so proud. I'm crying.

I remind her that she helped make it pos-sible, and text back: YOU should be proud too.

We exchange a few more texts. Dorie wants to talk, as do I, but she is on a set, working.

I carry the book back to my studio, trans-ferring it from one hand to the other; I like the weight of it. I sit at my desk and turn pages, stopping to admire photos of nineteenth-century bakers and candy factory workers. I read passages of Joy's clean clear prose. I run my fingers along the pages, my hand over the cover. I can't stop touching it, can't get enough proof that it is finally here, finally real.

On the back page — ABOUT THE AUTHOR — Joy's photo and bio. I can't stand the fact that it says she has died, seeing the reality of it in print, and that it says the book was "completed by her husband." I did not complete it; I helped shepherd it toward publication, and that's all.

I hold the book up and say, "All yours, honey."

As always, Joy does not answer. But maybe, just maybe, she knows.

It is a few weeks before the launch party and I have so much mixed emotion that I can't sort it out: a book party for Joy without Joy.

There is a lot to do. Coordinating with New York University is complicated, though Joy's friend and department chair in food studies, Jennifer Berg, is doing her best to keep me calm, not an easy job. Together, we visit and select an NYU venue. A few days later it's canceled due to scheduling conflicts. Another space is chosen. Then the invitation becomes problematic and difficult, several lists need to be collated: NYU's, Dorie's, Kathy's, mine. Dorie and I argue over the invitation's text, absurd, but we are both overly sensitive and stressed, trying to do everything perfectly while coordinating the artisanal food people Joy has written about in the last chapter of her book — many of whom have generously agreed to contribute to the event.

Another snafu: the second NYU venue selected only allows its own caterer to serve food. The indomitable Jennifer Berg once again steps in to explain these are only food purveyors who have been written about in the book. NYU relents. Another boulder moved off the road, a sigh of relief.

On the day of the launch I am absolutely sure no one will show up, a feeling I often have about my own parties, book readings, and events, but this one is more emotionally charged. I am also certain that several of the artisanal folk, who have promised to donate, will bail, or there will not be enough food and drink for the people I am convinced will not show up.

In the late afternoon I go to Amy's Bread in the Village to pick up a few loaves they are donating, and a miracle: they are bagged and waiting for me. Dorie is picking up from Bedford Cheese. Jennifer has already driven to Brooklyn and back for several cases of beer donated by Brooklyn Brewery. Her office tells me that Glorious Gin has sent the case of booze they promised and that several pounds of candy have arrived from Madelaine Chocolate.

Okay, we have beer, gin, candy, a few loaves of bread, and if Dorie is successful, a hunk of cheese. Not enough, I think, but maybe not an embarrassment.

With a poster-sized blowup of Joy's author photo tucked under one arm and the bag of Amy's Bread in the other I head over to NYU.

At Jennifer's office, I discover that neither Terra Chips nor Tom Cat Bakery has delivered anything. I text Dorie in a panic. She has not yet gone to Bedford Cheese but tells me to chill.

As if.

Jennifer and I walk over to NYU's Torch Club, which looks very much like its name, clubby and old-world, lots of wood and leather banquettes, the site of an old candy factory, something I know Joy would like. The only problem is that right now, one hour before countdown, the club is set up with a huge table to hold what I guess they imagine will be bucket loads of food, and the table fills more than half the room. We convince the staff to dismantle it. They do not look happy. I thank them over and over, smiling like an idiot. Soon, several small tables are set up around the room's perimeter. The bar is moved into a corner. I put Joy's picture near the entryway where they will be selling her book. I can barely look at it, so worried that I will disappoint her.

A case of Terra Chips arrives!

Next, Tom Cat Bakery delivers enough bread to feed a small village, and I am not exaggerating: loaf after loaf of every conceivable kind of bread, light, dark, white, rye, wheat, pumpernickel, oblong, round, rectangular, huge decorative loaves, plus 150 baguettes in individual bags to take away, along with Tom Cat employees to slice and hand out bread, two lovely young people, all smiles and aiming to please. It is beyond my wildest expectation.

Shamus Jones, creator and founder of Brooklyn Brine, shows up with jars of pickles to give away, plenty more for snacking.

Dorie arrives with platters from Bedford Cheese — assorted cheeses and packets of crackers, again more than either of us imagined.

The bar is stocked with wine and Brooklyn Brewery beer, and Jennifer is mixing dirty martinis with Glorious Gin and pickle juice from Brooklyn Brine. The small tables around the room are overflowing with bounty, a tribute to Joy.

The setup is not quite complete when people start arriving. Soon the club is full, crowded, well over a hundred people eating and drinking, the room buzzing.

Once or twice I am able to pull back from the throng and take it in — to see that it is actually happening. There is something slightly unreal about it, though I suspect I am the one who is unreal, feeling only semi-visible, there and not there as I meet and greet, an all too familiar feeling.

Speeches have been planned for the midway point, which sneaks up on me.

We have chosen the wide wooden stairway leading up to a second floor as a podium.

Jennifer Berg speaks first.

I stand among the crowd, watch, and listen as she talks of Joy, their friendship and professional relationship at NYU, Joy's book, which she is already reading. She is a great speaker, something Joy had always told me, and it's true; she not only says all the right things, but she is also funny and warm, her tribute deeply moving. Then Marion Nestle, Joy's colleague and a well-known food historian, takes Jennifer's place. She has written the introduction to *Food City,* and refused any payment. Her speech is an equally generous tribute.

My God, if only Joy could hear all of this. (Later, my cousin Nancy will tell me that she's sure Joy was there, and I decide to believe her.)

Then it's my turn.

I stand on the steps just slightly above the crowd. I take a deep breath. I thank a few people who need to be thanked. I say that *Food City* is *all* Joy's work, and how many years she devoted to it; I describe her office, her stacks of books and piles of research, the Post-its everywhere; I read the passage about her finding the pressed flowers inside the account book. I tell the assembled crowd that I'm sorry I ever told her to cut a single word. At one point I start to tear up, swallow hard, and abruptly switch gears to explain how Joy and I had side-by-side studios and our rule about not interrupting each other and how Joy obeyed the rule and I never did. People laugh. I thank my sister-in-law, Kathy, for her hard work and loaning me her shoulder to cry on; I say, "I understand why Joy chose her as a sister, such a good idea." More laughs. I thank my daughter. I say, "We did this as a family and I finally comprehend the meaning of that word, *family,* which goes far beyond the three of us." I raise a glass and say, "Here's to Joy." I thank everyone for coming, then hurry down the stairs and into the crowd. People tell me I did a good job, pat me on the back, and hug me. I nod and smile, a confluence of thoughts and emotion — pride for Joy, relief that the book is published, more relief the event is so clearly a success — all fused by incredible sadness.

Later, as the event wanes, Shamus Jones of Brooklyn Brine tells me how much he admired Joy and loved her, wells up with tears, and seeing this young Brooklyn hipster with tears in his eyes is almost too much for me. I tell him that Joy talked about him often and we had a running joke — that Joy had a crush on him. He looks down, blushing.

The guests take the baguettes home. I give the remaining Tom Cat loaves to the Torch Club staff.

I speak briefly with Dorie's ex-husband, Drew, and several of Dorie's friends, though Dorie has already made her escape, en route to the airport for a job in Los Angeles, something she debated — *Should I go, should I not?* — and I encouraged her (*Mom would want you to go*), a good excuse to flee the moment the event is over, enough emotional turmoil for one night.

At home, I feel a kind of exhaustion I have not felt since the months after Joy's death. Though the event was a success it had been even more draining than I'd imagined, though I'm not sure what I imagined. But I do not want to think about it. It was good, and it is over. An accomplishment. A milestone. So why can't I relax?

I get into bed and slide the laptop onto my chest. After a half hour, eyes almost closing, I turn it off and try to sleep but the book launch is still playing inside my head, along with all the worries that led up to it, as if none of them had been solved.

It takes me a while to realize that all of these things, these roadblocks and worries, were ways for me to evade the main thought that has been haunting every nook and cranny of my brain: the fact that Joy would not be at her book party, the fact that Joy is dead — a thought I could seldom get out of my mind, though one I had rarely acknowledged or wanted to, but tonight it has been unavoidable.

I sit up. I turn on the bedside lamp. I know that Joy would be annoyed with me, that she would tell me to stop ruining a good thing.

I tell her I'm sorry. I tell her that her book party was a great success.

I say, "You did it, honey," then I take a pill, turn out the light, and roll over.

41
GOING ON

Do we overcome grief?

The answer, for me, is not really. Grief is a permanent scar, part of who I am now and who I always will be. There are certain things we are not meant to get over and the loss of our nearest and dearest is, I believe, in that category. But it does not have to kill you (at least not yet).

Here is a contradiction that took me a long time to figure out: I desperately wanted to get past my grief but I also (subconsciously) dreaded it. Because getting past it might mean that all the reminders of Joy, and of our life together, would recede, or possibly even disappear, and I didn't want that to happen.

Grief is two-pronged: to get *past* it is to move on, a good thing; to get *over* it, to forget your grief and your former life and all that is attached to it, impossibly sad.

In the first year I was still buffered by

shock, but by the second year I had to accept the truth.

In the third year I have a sense of resignation: This is my life and I am (almost) used to it. I have good days and then not such good ones, stretches of time when I feel fine, then suddenly I do not. I still go out most nights, and occasionally pop a pill for sleep.

I no longer take for granted the relationship Joy and I had. Like many people I was caught up in my career, the minutiae of my life, the future. It's not as if those things went away, or that I don't care about them, I do, it's just that I am now aware of being caught up in them.

We were not the perfect couple, though I know some people projected that upon us. We argued, we disagreed (a lot), and we were both stubborn.

Because Joy and I talked about everything, and particularly *I* talked, I have so often wanted to tell Joy the things I miss about her, and how her death has affected me. Joy used to say, half-kidding, half not, "If I were suddenly gone you'd hardly notice."

Oh, honey, I notice.

Things I miss:

Going to the movies with Joy, something we did almost every week. When I didn't feel like going (Joy always wanted to), she would say, "You just have to sit there." I have been going to the movies again, with friends, sometimes alone, and it's okay. The other day I went to see one of those big comic book movies, which I like but Joy hated and I thought: *At least Joy is not suffering beside me.* Then I thought: *Too bad Joy is not suffering beside me.*

Seeing art. Having met in art school, Joy and I shared an intense love of art, of going to museums and galleries, and we had our own way of doing it: fast. We'd move quickly then stop, together, to look at a specific artwork, a few words exchanged but not much before moving on to the next piece that stopped us. There were only a handful of pieces in any show we really wanted to talk about and even then we didn't dwell on them, just expressed what we felt in a few succinct sentences before going on to the next. No one ever wanted to go to a museum with us, not if they'd gone with us before. Non–art lovers tend to linger over every piece — something I find excruciating — but Joy and I never dawdled. Trained at how to look at art, we knew what we wanted to see. There's hardly anyone I can do that with now except for Dorie on occasion, and one artist friend, so I tend to go to exhibits alone, and less often. When I do, I sometimes imagine Joy has stopped at exactly the same painting I have and we discuss (in my head) what it is that has stopped us. The other day I went to a contemporary museum show that's been getting a lot of attention, which I thought was basically crap. I was certain Joy would agree and I was sorry she was not there to commiserate. Disliking something is really only fun when there is someone else to dislike it with you.

Fancy restaurants. Joy adored them, loved ferreting out the newest and the best. I avoid them, dislike the pretension, find the idea of three minuscule, artfully arranged portions on a plate the size of a serving platter absurd. I guess this should be in the category of things I do *not* miss — though I miss complaining about going to them.

The other day, I took a walk with a friend, someone who knew me before and after Joy. At one point she said, "You finally seem like the 'full-spectrum Jonathan,'" and in some ways that's true, though I would say that I am a *different* full-spectrum Jonathan, and it made me think how and why, and what I've learned.

I learned that I am stronger in some ways and weaker in others, but not necessarily in the ways I once thought.

I learned that I love my work as much if

not more than ever. When I first lost Joy I felt that nothing mattered, particularly my work. But I've come full circle about that: I not only love my work, I *need* my work — my writing, my art, my teaching.

Something I am loath to admit: that the loss of my wife did not make me a stronger, better, or more enlightened person.

I recently read an essay by Ralph Waldo Emerson, "Experience," written two years after the death of his son, a reflection on loss and what grief does not deliver.

"The only thing grief has taught me," Emerson writes, "is to know how shallow it is. . . . I grieve that grief can teach me nothing."

I get that. In many ways we simply return to our former life, pick up the pieces, tape them back together, and move forward. I would amend Emerson's quote to say that I *have* learned from grief, learned that I can survive it, learned how to let in pain and loss, how to lower my mask, and how to confront my denial, though perhaps I am not necessarily the better for it.

I have to admit something else that is a bit more difficult: I like my freedom. I miss my wife and I miss our life together but I have grown accustomed to life alone, and I do not wish to start over with someone new.

Joy knew me, my life story, my fears, my needs, my hopes, my bullshit, and I have no desire to tell the story of my life to someone new. Even thinking about it exhausts me.

My daughter says I am constantly "workshopping" my life, trying to figure out what I want to do next, where I want to go or end up. And she's right. I think about selling my loft, about moving and traveling, about no longer teaching, and I talk about these things a lot though I'm still not sure. I have not moved and have essentially changed nothing, not Joy's McCoy pottery, nor my bedroom decor. And I still wear my wedding ring.

When people ask why, I say "because I like to," and that's the truth. I am used to it, like the weight of it on my finger, and of course it's a reminder of Joy. When people persist or say it's weird (and some actually do), I change the subject or turn the question around and ask them why they care. If that doesn't work I tell them it's none of their business.

Something else: In losing Joy I did not find God, but it opened something up in me, allowed my dormant spirituality to occasionally come to the fore. This past summer, in Assisi, Italy, I found myself kneeling at church altars, lighting candles, and saying silent prayers, an attempt, on my part, to make loss and death more tolerable.

Years ago, I'd gone to Japan to see the husband of a good friend who had died very suddenly and very young. He'd built an altar in their apartment, photographs of his late wife, my friend Michiko, several of which I had taken, along with artifacts from her life. Just moments after I walked in the door, he turned to the altar and said, "Michiko, Jonathan is here."

I can hardly remember another time I was so overwhelmed with feeling, and I never forgot it.

I have created my own modest altar in the living room of my loft — framed photos of Joy and Dorie, Joy with her parents, Joy and me, surrounded by a carved wooden statue of an unidentified saint, which Joy and I bought years ago in a junk shop; a small porcelain dish containing most of the stones and crystals Dorie and I got in Sonoma; a tacky figurine of Saint Francis, my favorite saint; a kitschy statuette of Santa Muerte, purchased in a Mexican flea market; a small blue painting of the artist Barnett Newman I made years ago that Joy loved; a tiny animal skull from Wyoming; Joy's favorite McCoy pot — a hodgepodge closer to kitsch than anything religious, though I rarely pass it without stopping and thinking of Joy. On occasion, I imagine Joy telling me to clean it up — she abhorred any sort of mess — but even that thought usually makes me smile.

I wonder if I still appear to be the "most unsentimental man, ever." Personally, I think my daughter got it wrong. I *am* a sentimental man, just one who eschews displays of sentiment, and those are two different things.

I still see that day with a kind of cinematic clarity, the paramedics in my loft, speeding through the streets of Manhattan, the hospital waiting room, everything about it charged and active. It's my movie, yet I remain on the edges of it, still and watching.

I am past the temporary madness of sudden loss and grief, no longer groping my way through a dark room.

What got me there?

Time. My daughter. Friends. Work.

A few nights ago I went to a dinner party, a dozen people at a long rectangular table. The host, a woman I have known for some time, the head of an arts organization, accomplished, smart, glamorous, had assembled an interesting group from the arts as well as business, and I knew many of them, one or two quite well.

It is a fun night, lots of talk that involves the entire table, not easy to do, but the host has a talent for engaging everyone.

Among the guests is a *New York Times* reporter, a young, vivacious woman, who tells the group how the writers in the *Times* Obituary Department refer to people as the "dead" and the "not yet dead." This produces a big laugh, and I laugh too though not as big or as loud because now that I have lost someone close to me I am no longer one of the people who thinks, *This is not going to happen to me.* There is more talk about the obits, how the newspaper stockpiles them for the famous and near-famous, which is still material for jest, and I see the humor in it too. We all live as if we are not going to die. How else could we live? Something I have come to understand more clearly these past three years.

I look around the table, not everyone is young, in fact a few people are closing in on elderly, surely they have lost people in their lives, but they are still joking about this thing called death. So am I, not exactly wisecracking but smiling at the various comments and jokes. How easy it would be to turn this into something serious, but in no way am I going to ruin this perfectly nice party nor would I want to.

I am relieved when the conversation turns to encounters with the ultrafamous and one of the women, one of the older ones, recounts a brief meeting with Marlon Brando. The host, who knows me well, urges me to tell my early teen encounter with Marilyn Monroe, when she had come to buy dresses at my father's company, and I do, including how the actress died three weeks later, the dresses never sent to her. It is a rather sad story, alleviated by the enduring fascination with Monroe the icon — *Was she beautiful? Was she nice? Was she troubled?* — but it is also one more tale that circles back to death. I'm happy when the next person tells a story of meeting Barack Obama almost a decade before he became president.

I am writing in my notebook late at night. It's warm and I have my studio windows open, a soggy breeze wafting in, carrying with it distant sirens and horns, nighttime sounds of the city, and music — a party happening somewhere in the warren of big and small buildings behind mine. For hours it's been rap and hip-hop, now it's a golden oldie, Dion and the Belmonts, "A Teenager in Love."

Joy and I had been dating only a month when we went to a party at a Boston club where a friend of mine was the DJ. He was a doo-wop and Motown freak — the Del Vikings, Five Satins, Gladys Knight and the Pips, Marvin Gaye. Joy and I arrived just as the Dion classic was booming through the speakers. Joy asked if I knew how to Lindy, and I did because my sister had taught me — we'd grown up watching *American Bandstand,* had studied the way those Philly kids danced, knew all the moves, and Joy did too. I led. Joy followed. Perfectly. It was as if we'd been dancing for years. Within minutes there was a circle around us, cheering us on — no one danced like that back then, partnered, *together,* so we were a novelty — and when the song changed to "Baby Love," we slowed down the same moves and that was it: the night we fell in love.

We could always impress a crowd with our Lindy skills, but it was never about anyone else, just about us, the way Joy anticipated my moves and I anticipated hers. I don't know about anyone else, but to me, dancing and sex are close relatives, and I think it's a damn shame that so many men don't dance because they don't know what they're missing. Over the many years we were married, there were times, at home, in the kitchen or living room, when a great song would come on the radio and I'd grab hold of Joy and we'd dance and fall in love all over again.

The next night I am on my way to dinner with a childhood friend of Joy's, someone I have known since before Joy and I married, though I haven't seen Judy in years.

We meet at a French restaurant on the Upper West Side, the kind of place that still serves coq au vin and sole meunière, almost everyone in the place of a certain age. I spot Judy immediately. She looks very much the way she did twenty-plus years ago, slim and cute, still a brunette, too young for this restaurant.

We start talking as if we have been chatting every day for years, Judy as funny and ironic as I remember. It is comforting to see her, a connection to Joy that goes even further back than my own.

We catch up on more recent history: Judy retired early from social work, is unmarried but in a long-term relationship.

In the middle of dinner I remember something. "Judy," I say. "It was *you* who asked Joy if she would hold your purse so you could dance."

"What?" Judy asks, confused. "When?"

"At our wedding."

"Really? I don't remember."

"Well, it wasn't significant, and a very long time ago."

"I'll say." Judy adds an eye roll, then more thoughtfully says, "You know, it's like you and Joy married so young that you missed growing up on your own so you have to do that now, experience all those things at this grown-up age."

I pick at my coq au vin and consider her comment before answering. "It's true, Joy and I *did* marry young, and we grew up together and experienced much of life together but . . . it's not entirely true either."

"How do you mean?"

"You know, the idea that a couple experiences *everything* together. You don't really. No matter how attached you are there are parts of yourself you never give away."

Judy nods with a knowing look.

"To some degree we're all alone, no matter how much we've shared — no matter how much we may believe that we are *not* alone there comes a time when we will be." I stop myself. "I'm sorry. I didn't mean to go off like that, to sound so pessimistic."

"It's fine," she says, "and I get it. Go on."

"It's just that losing Joy has made me consider my life, as a couple and my life alone. I don't necessarily see it as a new phase of my life, just a different one, and I'm trying to appreciate the differences. It's not just about starting a new life, it's about finding a place where I won't be restless, which I have always been and still am, though Joy helped keep me calm. I guess it's about finding that peaceful place on my own, which I have been trying to do."

"So you're okay?" she asks.

"Yes," I say. "I am."

Dinner over, Judy and I kiss good-bye and promise to stay in touch.

Seeing her has stirred up an array of emotions and memories.

I walk a few blocks, a montage of movie-like scenes toppling one over the other: sneaking Joy into my Boston University dorm room; pots and pans spread out to catch the rain in our leaky Hoboken loft; drying Dorie's tears on her first day of preschool, telling her it will be okay, and watching her put on a brave smile; the anniversary party just weeks before Joy died. I can feel myself working hard to replay the scenes with as much detail as possible, because *these*, among so many others, are the memories I want to preserve, along with the throwaway moments that cannot be described or named — the good stuff — as opposed to the nightmare images that have been haunting me for the past three years. They are, I realize, only a very small part of our life together, and we had a long one, longer than many, and that's what I want to remember.

ASHES

On a warm spring day, Dorie and I set out to do something we have been planning to do for three years.

I have Joy's ashes in small ziplock bags in one of the totes Dorie had made up for her amazingly successful Kickstarter campaign for Joy's book. The bag has the title of the book, **FOOD CITY**, printed on it in bold black letters. Also in the bag are photographs I have chosen, of Joy and me and Joy and Dorie, and some just of Dorie — as a baby, a toddler, a teen, a young woman. There are also pictures of Joy's mother and father and her sister, Kathy. In my other hand are a bunch of baby pink roses, Joy's favorite flower. Also in the tote is a tray I constructed out of balsa wood, very light and coated with an acrylic medium so it will withstand water, for a while. I have tested it in the sink and it seems okay.

Dorie has brought along some mementos

as well, but I have not asked her about them; they belong to her.

We head west from my loft toward the Hudson, toward the place along the river where Joy and I often took evening walks in spring, summer, and fall, to the place where Dorie and I also walked and sat and talked a few days after Joy died.

I feel a kind of wrenching sadness as I walk, Dorie beside me, emotions radiating from her like heat and static. We hold hands, the widower and his daughter, and we walk quickly, as if we have to be somewhere, as if we can't be late.

In the tote is a sealed envelope. Inside it, a letter I have written.

My darling Joy. I wish you could be with Dorie and me as we do this. You are the one thing, the one person, who is missing and it is all about you.

There are so many things I wish you could see.

I wish you could have seen how your cat, Lily, and I became devoted friends and companions.

I wish you could see how losing you has brought Dorie and me so close. I wish you could see how we talk about you (and how we still make fun of you, for which I apologize, though it is done only as a way to bring you closer to us, more vivid but in an everyday way. You know what I mean).

I wish you could see how your loss has brought me closer to Kathy. How I speak to your sister practically every day. And how we have all — Kathy and Dorie and I — worked so hard to make sure your book comes out in the world. I wish you were around to see that so much — your book, published. I am truly sorry about that. It's not fair. I picture you in your office, surrounded by books, working so hard, and how you deserve to know that it's happening, that it will be your legacy, your name on the cover, and your words, all of your work and research on every page, something people will be reading for a long time to come.

I wish you could have been with Dorie and me in all of the great restaurants in Mexico City, how you would have loved the food.

I wish you could see all the things your daughter does and accomplishes. I know how much it hurts her that you cannot, how often she wants to talk to you and how I am a poor substitute. There are certain things that a father can and cannot do, for which a mother, like you, is and was essential.

I wish you were around to celebrate any and all of the good things that happen for Dorie — and for me. Our accomplishments are less sweet by not having you to share them, the one person who was truly and completely always happy for us.

I wish you could see the drawings I've made of you. I think you'd like them.

I'm sorry for any and all of my failings — you know exactly what they were. But hey, I did my best, and you knew from the get-go what you were getting into, didn't you?

I never believed in an afterlife though I now want to believe you are sleeping peacefully, or gardening, or sitting in a great restaurant.

I want you to know that as I write this I am crying because you often accused me of being cold when it came to emotions and matters of the heart, but there have been moments during these past three years when I felt as if my heart were breaking in a literal way.

You were my anchor, a term I know you didn't like and found unsexy and unromantic, but I'm sorry to say you were. You kept me grounded.

We had a good time, didn't we? Most of

the time, I mean, right?

I want you to know I have gained weight and cannot get into my usual thirty-inch waist jeans. I know that will give you some pleasure.

I want you to know that Dorie and I are taking care of each other.

I want you to know that we are both doing okay.

We miss you. I miss you.

I love you.

Jonny

Dorie and I arrive at the chosen spot. It is just past midnight. Quiet. Almost deserted. Just a few people walking along the river's perimeter. We have to do this quickly. One, because we are not sure it's legal, and two, because we do not want to be interrupted.

Dorie and I are each saving a small portion of the ashes to keep. The rest we are about to offer up to the river and the wind.

I put the small dish I've brought into the small raft and add a portion of the ashes. I add the photos, half the pink roses, and my letter.

I ask Dorie if she wants to say anything and through her tears she says, "I love you, Mom," and places the things she has brought with her onto the tray.

We each take a ziplock bag of ashes and open it. I prepare Dorie by explaining it is not a powder, but a mix, coarse, with jagged pieces that I think might be bone. We each reach into the bags and take a handful.

I make sure we are upwind. I close my eyes and picture Joy, then toss them out toward the river. It's night but the city is never dark and I see them float on the water's surface. I follow with a few of the roses, which are more noticeable, so we can track the ashes more clearly.

Dorie does the same.

I release more ashes. I say more things to Joy inside my head.

I ask Dorie if she's ready to release the raft and she nods.

I manage to get it over the low wall and onto the river. I'm shocked it actually floats, and I'm thankful.

Dorie and I toss the rest of the roses in after it, and they too float on the river's dark, undulating surface.

We stand for a moment and watch, but we have decided ahead of time that we will not wait around to see the raft sink.

We turn away and hug.

Then I cry. I cry for the theft of Joy's old age and the time we should have had together, and cry for not being able to save her, and cry for my daughter's loss and my loss and all that Joy is missing. I cry because we never got to say good-bye, and cry because we will never again get to talk or laugh, or even cry together. I am no longer a man who cannot cry. I am a man who cannot stop crying.

Dorie and I separate, though we are still holding hands, and head away from the river toward home.

I want to look back but I think that Joy would tell me it is enough. We did it. The river and the wind will do the rest.

ACKNOWLEDGMENTS

Clearly, this was a difficult time in my life and there are many people to thank for making it less so.

My magnificent friends: Jane O'Keefe, Jane Kent, and David Storey, who were there for me in every possible way; Susan Crile and Jane Rivkin, both of whom housed me, fed me, and nurtured me with their generosity and kindness. Judd Tully, who was available from day one, along with Ben Bunch, my exemplary young pal, wise and kind beyond his years; Kira Nam Greene, Stewart Wallace, Dan Conaway, Tolga and Pemra Ornek, Megan Abbott, David Falk, Noreen Tomassi, Honor Molloy and Joseph Goodrich, Nancy and Don Graff, Bruce and Micheline Ektin, Michele Leblond, and the many friends who made me feel less alone by staying in touch and showing up.

My dear friend Caren Cross, whom I miss every day; likewise, my friend Jack Rivkin.

My brilliant bud, S. J. Rozan, who read versions of this book, offered her expertise and notes on grammar without ever implying I was illiterate.

Joyce Carol Oates, an invaluable cheerleader and friend, who understands the nature of loss, encouraged me to write this book and believed I could.

Elaina Richardson, who opened her home and her heart, who was the first person to read parts of this book and say: *YES!*

The Corporation of Yaddo, for time, space, and sanctuary; and Candace Wait, who encouraged me to leave my New York City apartment when I did not think I could.

Pat Towers, for her unwavering spirit, who read and edited the first full draft, who told me what was right and what was wrong (though she never used those words).

Janice Deaner, Rachel Shteir, Beena Kamlani, writers and friends, who read, listened, and offered invaluable suggestions.

Eva Orner, to whom I will be forever grateful for her introduction to Todd Shuster of Aevitas Creative, a true gentleman and scholar, and Jane von Mehren, who edited drafts of this book with a keen eye, brilliant ear, and kind heart.

Kathryn Court, the kind of publisher one

dreams of and rarely gets. Victoria Savanh, Louise Braverman, and the terrific team at Penguin Books — this book would not exist without them.

My nephew Michael Lodish, for his help and love balanced by his ridiculous sense of humor (which I share); and my sister, Roberta, for listening. My mother, Edith, for her beautiful speech about Joy and for being the best mom one could ever imagine. My sister-in-law, Kathy Rolland, who provided a shoulder and an ear and to whom I whine almost as much as I did to Joy (possibly more, because she is not married to me).

And to my beautiful, brilliant, and talented daughter, Doria, who made it possible for me to go forward and who makes it all matter.

ABOUT THE AUTHOR

Jonathan Santlofer is a writer and artist. His debut novel, *The Death Artist,* was an international bestseller, translated into seventeen languages, and is currently in development for screen adaptation. His fourth novel, *Anatomy of Fear,* won the Nero Award for best novel of 2009. His short stories have appeared in numerous anthologies. He is also the creator and editor of several anthologies including *It Occurs to Me That I Am America,* a collection of original stories and art. His paintings and drawings are included in many public and private collections. He lives in New York City.